low-salt cooking

low-salt cooking

OVER 70 RECIPES PROVIDE HEALTHY
AND TASTY SOLUTIONS TO COOKING
WITHOUT SALT

CONTRIBUTING EDITOR:
MICHELLE BERRIEDALE-JOHNSON

LORENZ BOOKS

This edition is published by Lorenz Books

Lorenz Books is an imprint of Anness Publishing Ltd
Hermes House, 88–89 Blackfriars Road, London SE1 8HA
tel. 020 7401 2077; fax 020 7633 9499
www.lorenzbooks.com; info@anness.com

© Anness Publishing Ltd 1999, 2003

UK agent: The Manning Partnership Ltd, 6 The Old Dairy, Melcombe Road, Bath BA2 3LR;
tel. 01225 478444; fax 01225 478440; sales@manning-partnership.co.uk

UK distributor: Grantham Book Services Ltd, Isaac Newton Way, Alma Park Industrial Estate, Grantham, Lincs NG31 9SD;
tel. 01476 541080; fax 01476 541061; orders@gbs.tbs-ltd.co.uk

North American agent/distributor: National Book Network, 4501 Forbes Boulevard, Suite 200, Lanham, MD 20706;
tel. 301 459 3366; fax 301 429 5746; www.nbnbooks.com

Australian agent/distributor: Pan Macmillan Australia, Level 18, St Martins Tower, 31 Market St, Sydney, NSW 2000;
tel. 1300 135 113; fax 1300 135 103; customer.service@macmillan.com.au

New Zealand agent/distributor: David Bateman Ltd, 30 Tarndale Grove, Off Bush Road, Albany, Auckland;
tel. (09) 415 7664; fax (09) 415 8892

A CIP catalogue record for this book is available from the British Library

Publisher: Joanna Lorenz
Editor: Margaret Malone
Designer: Julie Francis
Editorial Reader: Joy Wotton
Production Controller: Joanna King
Photographers: Karl Adamson, Steve Baxter, James Duncan, Ian Garlick, Michelle Garrett, Amanda Heywood, Dave
Jordan, Don Last, William Lingwood, Patrick McLeavey, Thomas Odulate, David Reilly
Recipes: Catherine Atkinson, Angela Boggiano, Carla Capalbo, Kit Chan, Jacqueline Clark, Trish Davies, Nicola Diggins,
Matthew Drennan, Sarah Edmonds, Joanna Farrow, Christine France, Silvana Franco, Shirley Gill, Rebekah Hassan,
Manisha Kanani, Lesley Mackley, Norma Macmillan, Sue Maggs, Norma Miller, Sallie Morris, Steven Wheeler,
Kate Whiteman, Jeni Wright

Previously published as *Healthy Eating Library: The Low-salt Cookbook*

1 3 5 7 9 10 8 6 4 2

NOTES
For all recipes, quantities are given in both metric and imperial measures and,
where appropriate, measures are also given in standard cups and spoons.
Follow one set, but not a mixture, because they are not interchangeable.

Standard spoon and cup measures are level.
1 tsp = 5ml, 1 tbsp = 15ml, 1 cup = 250ml/8fl oz

Australian standard tablespoons are 20ml. Australian readers should
use 3 tsp in place of 1 tbsp for measuring small quantities of gelatine,
cornflour, salt, etc.

Medium eggs are used unless otherwise stated.

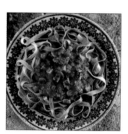

Contents

INTRODUCTION

It may seem difficult to believe that salt, which is now so cheap and so universally available, was once a rare and highly prized mineral. But so it was – just think of expressions such as "worth his salt" or "the salt of the earth". And there was good reason for valuing salt so highly. Salt was, and still is, crucial to the successful functioning of human society for two main reasons. The first is that it is vital to the healthy functioning of the body, although the amount needed to make the body function efficiently is tiny compared to the amount that most of us actually eat, and the second is that, until recent times, salting was one of the very few ways in which food could be successfully preserved. We now know, however, that salt is not such a benign presence in our lives.

WHAT IS SALT?

Salt, or sodium chloride, to give it its chemical name, is a mineral made up of approximately 40 per cent sodium and 60 per cent chloride. Depending on where the salt comes from, it may also include around 1 per cent of other trace minerals.

Salt does occur naturally in foods – mainly in meat and fish – but in much smaller quantities than the amount that we normally consume. A few vegetables, such as celery, beetroot, spinach and watercress, also contain salt, but the majority of vegetables and cereals are virtually salt free. The ones that do contain salt carry it in an organic form, which means that it

is contained in a living organism – the vegetable – rather than in an inorganic, or pure mineral, form. The organic form is thought to be more easily and more usefully assimilated by the body.

All the salt that we eat came originally from the sea. On average a litre of sea water contains around 25g of salt, which means that the oceans provide us with a bottomless reservoir of salt. However, the vast majority of the salt in commercial use, rock salt, is mined from the beds of ancient seas, now far inland, which have long since drained away. Sea salt is gathered from coastal deposits – and, in some cases, evaporated from the sea itself.

Above: Sea salt (left) and rock salt. Both are obtainable for culinary use, but sea salt is less widely available.

FOOD PRESERVATION

Salt has the ability to draw water or liquid out of any matter – or foodstuff – to which it is applied. This property inhibits bacterial growth within food, as long as it remains in contact with the salt.

This discovery was the first crucial step in food preservation. In the days before freezers, cans and vacuum packs, this was an enormously important and significant discovery. It meant that food could be preserved from the season of plenty and growth to the season of want. Meat and fish, for example, could be preserved over the winter, thus ensuring communities a regular supply of food throughout the year. It also meant that human beings could travel more freely and widely, as they could now carry preserved food stocks with them, in case none was to be found as they

Left: Foods such as meat and fish, and a few vegetables, like spinach, celery and watercress, naturally contain salt.

moved. This was to be of huge significance right up until the 20th century, especially for sea travel.

Using large quantities of salt to preserve food did however, have the gastronomic disadvantage that most foods tasted very salty. Lengthy cooking was often needed to try to reduce its saltiness. Salt cod, for example, might need to be boiled for 12 hours just to render it edible. Even so, people's taste buds became so accustomed to salted foods that low-salt or saltless foods tasted bland – thus encouraging the use of added salt as a seasoning even in foods that had not been salted for preservation.

A VALUABLE COMMODITY

The ability of salt to purify and to preserve quickly turned it into a valuable commodity, both financially and spiritually. Throughout the ancient world, salt rapidly became the single most important traded commodity. The wealth of cities such as Venice was built on their salt trade, while salt trading routes criss-crossed Europe and the East.

Salt acquired a "purifying" significance in religions across the world. The ancient Greeks believed salt to be the gift of the gods; the Romans offered it on their altars with incense; and the Hebrews sprinkled every offering to God with salt.

Salt was also a symbol of hospitality and a measure of wealth. Rents were paid in salt, taxes were levied in salt. Indeed, the *gabelle*, or salt tax, was said to be the final straw that sparked off the French Revolution.

From the earliest times, craftsmen laboured to create salt cellars or salt containers from gold, silver and precious stones, which celebrated both the value of the salt itself – and the wealth of its owner.

Right: Equipment for traditional pie- and jam-making laid out on the table, including a substantially large pillar of salt.

THE PRE-HISTORY OF SALT

Our prehistoric ancestors (the hunter gatherers) lived on a mainly animal diet, so they would easily have absorbed the 2.5g of salt (1g sodium) that they needed daily from the meat that they ate. Today, the Inuits – who live almost entirely on fish – continue to obtain necessary amounts of salt from the fish and the Bedouins obtain their salt from drinking large quantities of milk.

Around 4000 BC, Neolithic people began to settle in one place and learned how to grow and cook food. Their diet changed to include more vegetables and cereals, both of which carry small to negligible amounts of salt. At more or less the same time, they invented cooking pots that were strong enough to allow them to boil food in water – which is a far more convenient way to cook than roasting, but which leaches the salt out of the food into the water. All of a sudden, their diet became virtually saltless and for reasons of both health and flavour, they needed to replace that salt.

The earliest known salt mines dating from this Neolithic period are in Hallstatt near Salzburg (meaning salt city) in Austria, although there are over a dozen other Neolithic salt mines in Europe, plus a further four sites where salt was extracted from the sea.

THE ROLE OF SALT IN GOOD HEALTH

The human body is over 60 per cent water. This fluid is to be found in the blood, the lymphatic system and the cells of the body. Sodium, together with chloride, potassium and phosphate, control the amount of fluid within and outside the cells of the body, keeping them evenly balanced. Maintaining this balance is absolutely essential to the body's proper functioning.

DIETARY FACTORS: TOO MUCH SODIUM

It is estimated that the average person, in average conditions, requires less than 1g of sodium (which equals around 2.5g of salt) per day for proper bodily function. Yet in the Western world current research estimates that the average person eats 10–15g of salt (4–6g of sodium) a day – which is between five and ten times more than they need.

Unlike in the case of, say, vitamin C, we do not excrete the salt we do not need, so any excess gets absorbed into our body fluids. If excess sodium appears in the blood, in order to reduce its sodium concentration to normal, water will be drawn out of cells into the blood to dilute it. If yet more salt is eaten (and consequently, more sodium is deposited in the blood), the body will crave more fluid to dilute the excess of sodium – in other words, you will get thirsty.

This will cause you to carry excess fluid – up to several litres, which will put a strain on the vascular system and the heart. This is a common cause of high blood pressure.

TOO LITTLE SODIUM

Insufficient sodium, although rare, is just as dangerous as excess sodium and it will also unbalance the body's systems. Symptoms include cramps and aching muscles, lassitude, anorexia, vomiting and mental confusion.

Shortage of sodium will normally only affect those who sweat a great deal, as they excrete sodium along with their sweat. This may be because of continuous exercise, for example, or due to heavy manual labour, or because people are living in a climate to which they are not adapted, as with white-skinned northerners living in the tropics. In either case, they may need to take extra salt to replace the sodium lost in their sweat.

POTASSIUM

Potassium is one of the other vital minerals needed by the body to maintain its fluid balance and there is a good deal of evidence to suggest that high-sodium diets result in an excess loss of potassium. There is also evidence to suggest that the high blood pressure associated with excess sodium intake can sometimes be reduced by an increased consumption of potassium, which is easily available from fruits and vegetables. This may explain, at least in part, why many vegetarians, with their higher intake of potassium-rich fruits and vegetables, such as avocado, bananas and nuts, are less likely to have high blood pressure.

Extra potassium can also be obtained by using a high-potassium salt alternative, now readily available.

Left: Shortage of sodium (found in salt) is usually a problem only for people who exercise strenuously for long periods.

Left: A diet containing fruit, vegetables and unsalted nuts will be rich in potassium.

CORONARY HEART DISEASE

High blood pressure is also closely related to our chances of suffering from coronary heart disease. This happens when the arteries taking blood to and from the heart get clogged with cholesterol deposits, making it difficult for the heart to pump the blood through them.

Although the level of fat in the diet and the blood, and the blood's natural "stickiness" or tendency to clot are also relevant in this process, high blood pressure is recognized to be an important contributory factor. Since nearly 30 per cent of deaths in the Western world are caused by coronary heart disease, all factors are important.

OSTEOPOROSIS

There is now a good deal of evidence to suggest that a high intake of salt/sodium causes the body to excrete calcium from the bones through the urine. This calcium loss reduces bone density which, if it goes on for long enough, will lead to osteoporosis, loss of height and mobility, and possibly complex fractures. Apart from the suffering and medical expense involved, such fractures in the elderly can often lead to fatal complications.

CANCER

There is some evidence to connect an excessive intake of sodium with cancer of the stomach and of the naso pharynx. Although this evidence is not conclusive, the World Cancer Research Fund – which recently conducted a massive review of cancer research and made wide-ranging dietary recommendations – has suggested that salt consumption should be limited to a maximum of 6g/¼oz salt (2.4g/¹⁄₁₆oz of sodium) per day.

Some methods for treating cancer through diet forbid the addition of any salt as part of the therapy.

HIGH BLOOD PRESSURE

There is now a convincing body of scientific evidence to suggest that a higher intake of salt/sodium increases the amount of water in the body. This puts pressure on the veins and the ability of the heart to pump the blood through them, in turn causing blood pressure to rise and the individual to suffer from high blood pressure, or hypertension.

This evidence also suggests that, in Western societies, the effect of excess salt/sodium is cumulative. In other words, the longer we continue eating too much salt (i.e. the older we get), the higher our blood pressure will get. Research shows that, in non-Western societies where people consume a diet that is lower in salt, blood pressure does not rise with age.

Although it could be argued that there are other lifestyle factors that might influence the health patterns of non-Western societies, the same relation of low-salt diet and low blood pressure can be seen in animals such as chimpanzees.

STROKE

By the late 19th century, salt consumption had reached a peak and it is estimated that the average person may have been eating as much as 20g/¾oz per day. Although exact records do not exist, apoplexy (or stroke) was one of the major causes of death at this time.

There is now a vast body of medical and scientific evidence to show that high blood pressure is the strongest predictive factor for a stroke. In other words, high blood pressure is the one physical condition which is more likely to make you have a stroke than any other.

Strokes account for around 10–12 per cent of all deaths in the Western world. In addition to these fatal strokes, over 20 per cent of the Western population will suffer from non-fatal strokes, which none-the-less cause enormous suffering to those who are partially or totally paralysed, either physically or mentally, and huge financial and emotional costs to those caring for them.

WHY WE EAT SO MUCH SALT

The arrival of freezing and canning techniques means that we now need very little salt to preserve our food, so how is it that we are still consuming well over 10g more salt a day than we need? Have our taste buds become so accustomed to salt that we are adding it to everything we eat to give it "flavour"? Or has the nature of our food changed so much that it provides us with this extra salt whether we wish it to or not? The answer is probably a bit of both.

THE IMPACT OF NEW TECHNOLOGIES ON SALT LEVELS IN FOOD

Thanks to massive advances in food technology since World War II, the vast majority of what the average person eats and drinks today in the Western world has already been processed. Even food that we see as relatively

Below: Salt is often added during the canning process, so always choose fresh products whenever possible.

"natural", such as fruit juices, has been processed in some way to preserve it or make it taste "better".

There is no doubt that many of the techniques used involve a liberal use of salt. This means that whether or not we choose to add extra salt to the food we eat, we still often consume large quantities of it every day. Even when we cook for ourselves, many of the ingredients that we use may already have been manufactured and therefore contain relatively high levels of salt.

WHY DO MANUFACTURERS USE SO MUCH SALT?

The answer probably boils down to one word – money. Because of its abundance, salt is now a cheap commodity on the world food market. It is far cheaper as a seasoning than herbs or any other ingredients that can be used to give flavour to a dish.

Due to its hydroscopic qualities – its ability to draw water to itself – salt can also be used to add water to certain products, such as meat. If the meat is

high in salt, it can be injected with water, which, because of the nature of the salt, it will retain – thus making the meat heavier than it would otherwise be.

Excess salt makes people thirsty, which means that they need to drink more, which often means processed fizzy or packaged drinks. These are not infrequently made by the same company as the one that made the salty foods – so thirst is good for business, too.

Manufacturers claim that, since the food-buying public want to buy food as economically as possible (most people see price rather than quality as the most important criterion when choosing food), it is their responsibility to make it as cheaply as possible. Using a cheap flavouring ingredient or using salt to increase the water content of some foods to increase bulk and make them cheaper, is therefore justifiable. It should also be said, however, that using cheap ingredients, or those which increase the weight of a product at very little expense to themselves, also allows manufacturers and processors to make larger profits on those foods.

Obviously, processing varies enormously but it is not unusual for the processed variety of a food to have up to 20 times more salt/sodium than the fresh variety – a canned vegetable

Above: Many everyday ingredients have high levels of "hidden" salt: for example, stock cubes, baking powder and hard and pre-sliced cheeses.

or fruit as opposed to a fresh one, for example, bread as opposed to flour, or bacon as opposed to pork.

Manufacturers are becoming aware of increasing concern over the amount of salt/sodium in their products, and some are already developing low-salt versions of certain dishes. Others are starting gradually to reduce the amount of salt that they use in products such as bread. However, there is still a long way to go, and anyone who is concerned about the amount of salt they eat should make themselves familiar with those manufactured foods that are likely to have the highest salt/sodium levels.

Left: Commercially produced sauces, such as soy, ketchup, barbecue and pastes, such as anchovy, can contain relatively large amounts of salt.

SOME KEY INGREDIENTS CONTAINING HIGH LEVELS OF SALT

- stock cubes or bouillon
- baking powders, baking sodas and other chemical raising agents
- many commercial sauces, such as Worcestershire, anchovy, brown, soy, ketchup, etc.
- spreads and salted butters
- canned meats and processed meats, such as bacon and ham
- canned fish
- canned vegetables
- breadcrumbs
- cheese, particularly pre-sliced cheese and many hard cheeses

HIGH-SALT MANUFACTURED FOODS

When you are assessing how much salt there is in a dish, remember that the current recommendation is that the average person should eat no more than 6g/¼oz of salt (2.4g/¹⁄₁₆oz of sodium) per day. If you are on a specifically low-salt diet, you will have been given an even lower target by your doctor. When considering your salt intake, you may be horrified to discover how many dishes will provide you with as much as 3g/⅛ oz of salt (half your daily allowance) in just one dish.

ASSESSING SALT LEVELS IN MANUFACTURED FOODS

Because the ingredients of individual dishes vary enormously, the list below is a guide only to manufactured or processed foods and dishes that you might expect to contain excess salt. You should always read the nutrition labels carefully to make quite sure that you know how much salt/sodium there is in that particular version.

Unfortunately, though, the labels won't always help you. A large number of the foods listed here, even when they do give a nutritional breakdown on the pack, do not include salt in that breakdown.

FOODS CONTAINING ADDED SALT

A surprising number of manufactured foods contain salt, the most common ones being listed below:
- breakfast cereals
- breads, especially flavoured ones
- biscuits, both sweet and savoury
- salted butters and spreads

- hard cheeses, such as Cheddar, Cheshire, Parmesan and Pecorino, Gruyère, Gouda, Edam, Samsoe, Havarti and Jarlsberg
- soft cheeses, such as ricotta or mozzarella, should not have such a high salt content, though some of the manufactured cheese slices may have more than you expect
- savoury snacks, such as crisps, cheesy biscuits, salted crackers, Twiglets and salted nuts

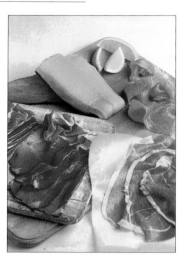

- bacon and ham, Parma ham
- all smoked meats
- ready meals, including both meat and vegetable dishes
- many ready-made pasta dishes, such as lasagne, cannelloni and macaroni cheese
- pizzas

- sandwiches – it may be difficult to tell how much salt is in a sandwich as the label will not usually detail all the ingredients of the bread or spread used, but you can usually assume that it will be high
- soups, whether canned, fresh, frozen or dried
- all smoked fish
- all ready-made fish dishes, including fish pies, fish pastes and pâtés, spreads such as taramasalata, and fish fingers and fish cakes

- pies of any kind, including pork pies, Cumberland pies, shepherd's pie, Cornish pasty
- burgers of any kind, meat or vegetarian
- sausages, sausage rolls, salami
- ready-made flans and quiches
- ready-made Chinese meals, which can contain monosodium glutamate
- ready-made Indian meals
- canned vegetables, including baked beans
- salad dressings
- sauces, including ketchups and soy sauces

- commercial desserts and cakes
- even drinks can contain processing agents, which may be based on, or contain, sodium

THE IMPORTANCE OF NUTRITIONAL LABELS

The most obvious way to reduce your intake of ready-made dishes is to cook for yourself – which is what the recipe section of this book is all about. Although cooking all your own food may be the ideal, most people will be only too glad to find a few ready-made dishes that they can still buy. To be able to do so with an easy mind, however, reading the nutritional tables is essential.

As the law stands at the moment, the manufacturers are only required to list the ingredients on the packaging of any product. These ingredients have to be listed in descending order of quantity. In other words, the ingredient of which there is the most has to appear first in the list and so on, down to the ingredient which appears in the smallest quantity. Unfortunately, however, manufacturers do not have to specify exactly how much of each ingredient is in the dish. Also unfortunately, the regulations only apply to the major ingredients in a dish, not to flavourings such as salt.

There is also something called the "25 per cent rule on compound ingredients". This means that if any part of a dish or a food makes up less than 25 per cent of the whole dish (like the dressing in a salad sandwich), the manufacturer does not have to give the ingredients of that part. In other words, you will not be able to tell from the label whether there is any salt in the dressing at all, let alone how much.

No product is currently required to carry a nutritional table, although many do – especially ready-made meals. However, if there is a nutritional table, you should be better informed. If it is a full table, it will give you the sodium content of both 100g/3½oz of the food concerned and of a portion.

This is not entirely ideal, as to learn the salt content of a dish requires some calculations. To find your salt intake, you have to multiply the sodium content by 2.5.

The reason why the table gives the sodium, rather than the salt, content of the food is that it is the sodium that is the active compound that raises blood pressure. This is not helpful, however, for the average shopper who thinks in terms of salt, not sodium. Consumer groups are pressing for the regulations governing salt/sodium declarations to be changed so that labels also include the relevant figure for salt to make the table easier to understand.

The chances are, however, that a large number of foods that you might wish to buy will use a "shorter" form of the nutritional table, which may not include a sodium declaration at all. In that case, if your salt intake is not too critical, you should use the guide on the left to avoid high-sodium foods. And if you are on a strict low-salt diet, you should avoid any ready-made food that does not give you details of its salt/sodium contents.

Finally, bear in mind that any ingredient that includes the word "sodium" – such as sodium bicarbonate – will contain sodium, even in the most unlikely place (a sweet fizzy drink, for example) and even if it is only in a small quantity.

USING THE NUTRITION NOTES IN THIS BOOK
Every recipe in this book comes with its own nutritional breakdown so that you can quickly and easily see the sodium intake per portion. Remember that the recommended daily amount of sodium for an average person watching their salt intake is 1g (1000mg), or 2.5g of salt.

REDUCING THE SALT IN YOUR COOKING

The long-term advantage of any special diet is that it forces you to cook more for yourself at home. Initially this may seem like a terrible punishment, but many people find that once they start they really enjoy more adventurous cooking, and that the health benefits they derive from eating fresh food which also agree with their dietary requirements are well worth the bit of extra work.

Apart from experimenting with new dishes and flavours, such as those in the recipe section, there are also a few general principles that you can apply to all your cooking.

ADDING LESS SALT

There was a time when no one would ever think of eating a meal without sprinkling salt and pepper on it before they even tasted it. But although this practice has now all but disappeared, many people still cannot imagine cooking potatoes or pasta without salt in the water, making a sauce without a shake of salt "for flavour", roasting a joint without salting the outside, or not adding a pinch of salt to their egg whites when making meringues. In fact, none of these practices is necessary – they are merely habit.

Vegetables have plenty of flavour of their own, which is only masked by putting a lot of salt in the cooking water – although because it is in the nature of salt to leach out of the food into the water rather than from the water into the food, salted cooking water makes for far less salty food than salting the dish itself.

Like any other flavouring – sugar is the prime example – you can always add more to your dish, but you cannot take it out once it is in. As the salt intake decreases, it is amazing how quickly our tastebuds will adapt to a less salty diet and you will suddenly start to discover all kinds of other exciting flavours which have previously been masked by the salt.

Unless you have been told to cut salt out of your diet entirely, reduce the amount of salt that you use gradually: this way, you will scarcely notice.

Above: You can still enjoy vegetables without adding salt during cooking: simply rub them with a little salted butter.

REDUCING YOUR SALT INTAKE GRADUALLY

Taste your food before adding salt, and only add just as much as you really need to make it acceptable. Measure out the amount of salt you would normally use for any dish, then reduce it by 25 per cent. Two weeks later, reduce the new amount that you are using by a further 25 per cent, and so on, until you use none at all. This will allow your taste buds to adapt gradually to the more varied flavours of less salty foods.

Use salt carriers rather than salt itself. For example, if you cannot bear the thought of a boiled egg without salt, add a tiny bit of salted butter to the egg rather than straight salt – you will end up with less salt but still a good flavour.

Similarly, if you cannot bear not to have salt on your vegetables, lightly rub them with a little salted butter when cooked rather than sprinkling them with salt itself.

HOME-MADE BREAKFAST CEREAL

You will find this nutritious cereal far tastier – and healthier – than any ready-made version.

INGREDIENTS

Makes 1 large bowl
90ml/6 tbsp raw rolled oats
15ml/1 tbsp each unsalted sunflower, pumpkin and sesame seeds
30ml/2 tbsp each unsalted flaked almonds, walnuts and hazelnuts
15ml/1 tbsp wheatgerm
15ml/1 tbsp each dried fruit, such as raisins, sultanas, currants, figs, dates

To serve
fresh fruit, such as bananas, apples, peaches, pears
milk, or yogurt, or fruit juice

1 In a large, clean bowl combine all the dry ingredients and mix thoroughly together.

2 Adjust the quantities of the dry ingredients to suit your taste, then make up enough for a week before storing in a clean, airtight container. When serving, add fresh fruit of your choice and milk.

LOW-SALT COOKING METHODS

Just as water leaches salt out of food, so it leaches out the food's flavour too. Using less water in your cooking will therefore also conserve the natural flavour of food. Cooking any composite dish in its own juices will help retain all the flavour, rather than throwing it out with the cooking water.

STIR-FRYING

- An excellent way to cook finely slivered meats, fishes or vegetables with the minimum fat and salt is to stir-fry them in a wok or large frying pan. Add flavour with herbs and spices, such as garlic, ginger, cumin, lemon juice, mustard seeds, seasoned vinegars and flavoured stir-fry oils.
- Avoid soy sauce and other similar sauces, which are high in salt.

ROASTING/BAKING

- Roasting meats concentrates the flavour by drying them out. They should not need any further seasoning, but you could help them along by sitting them on an appropriate herb – rosemary for lamb, say, sage for pork, horseradish root for beef, tarragon for chicken – or by inserting slivers of garlic into slits in the flesh.

- Larger fish can be successfully roasted or baked either whole or in cutlets. Wrapping fish in foil helps to retain the juices, especially for cutlets or fillets. Add flavouring with lemon slices, dill weed, tarragon or fennel.
- Any combinations of vegetables – both root and leaf – can be roasted together. Lay them in a baking tray with a little olive oil and the herb – dry or fresh – of your choice.

STEAMING

- You can buy an inexpensive steamer from any kitchen shop, and steam all your vegetables rather than boiling them. This is particularly good for root vegetables, such as potatoes, sweet potatoes, carrots, celeriac, beetroot, parsnips and turnips, which will steam in 10–20 minutes, depending on the vegetable and how thick the slices are. Leaf vegetables such as cabbage, sprouts and spinach also steam well, and they are less likely to become soggy cooked in this way. Other vegetables that will benefit from steaming include cauliflower, peas and beans.
- Fish is excellent steamed because this is a far gentler method than poaching or boiling, which tends to break up the flesh. Some meats can be steamed, too, but be sure to use the steaming water in the sauce.

MICROWAVING

- Cook your vegetables in the microwave in a couple of tablespoons of water or stock. Meat works well in the microwave, too, as it retains its juices, though it does not therefore concentrate the flavour quite as well as roasting, which tends to dry out the meat. Fish can be microwaved in a small amount of liquid.
- The microwave is also good for steamed desserts, such as steamed marmalade or treacle pudding.

GRILLING/BARBECUING

- Anything that can be roasted can also be grilled or barbecued. As with roasting, the flavour is concentrated as the food dries out under the influence of the direct heat.
- Herbs placed with the food add flavour, as does marinating it in herbs, spices, chopped fruits, lemon juice, wine or olive oil beforehand.

ALTERNATIVE FLAVOURINGS

There are many alternative ingredients and flavourings that are healthier and tastier than the processed variety. Review the ingredients that you use normally and see where you could substitute a lower-salt version. However, remember that some high-salt ingredients (cheese and smoked fish, for example) contain other important health-giving nutrients, such as calcium and omega 3 fatty acids, so you may want to weigh that up against other high-salt but less nutritious ingredients.

If you don't have time to prepare home-made stock, a quick alternative is a mixture of wine and water.

Choose wholemeal ingredients when possible. The distinctive flavour of brown rice, for example, requires no added salt.

For cooking use virgin oils, which are naturally salt-free and are beneficial to health in other ways too.

STOCK

Most commercial bouillon cubes are notoriously high in salt, so replace them, wherever possible, with home-made stock. This is easy to prepare and can be "stockpiled" by making a large batch and then freezing it in small quantities for future use.

You could also replace the stock altogether by using a mixture of water and wine – replacing 10-25 per cent of the total amount of liquid with wine (red or white depending on the dish) and the rest with water.

Salt-free/no-salt-added stock cubes are available if you really don't have time to make your own stock.

WHOLEMEAL INGREDIENTS

Use wholemeal ingredients (flour, rice, etc.) whenever possible. They have much more natural flavour than the white, highly processed version of the same food. If you think that they will make the resulting dish too heavy (if using only wholemeal flour in baking, for example) then use half wholemeal and half white.

Bakes such as wholemeal pitta breads, scones, muffins and teacakes make a good, high fibre snack or treat. Choose wholemeal or whole grain varieties whenever possible or make your own bakes at home using wholemeal flour and adding extra dried fruit. Serve bakes such as scones or muffins plain or with a little low-fat spread, honey or reduced-sugar jam for a delicious, filling snack.

OILS

Use oils rather than butter or spreads for all your cooking and baking. Oils are naturally saltless, while spreads and butters can have quite a high salt content. Virgin oils such as olive or sunflower as a cooking medium, for example, will be much better for your overall health. If you do use butter, make sure you buy the saltless variety.

SALAD DRESSINGS

Substitute a little oil and vinegar or oil and lemon juice, two grinds of pepper and a shake of a low-sodium salt for commercial salad dressings, which are nearly always high in salt.

Below: It takes only a few seconds to prepare your own healthy salad dressing using just a little low-sodium salt or with no salt at all.

SAUCES

If you use ready-prepared sauces or ketchups, find the version which has the least salt – and cut down gradually on its use. If you start using other flavourings, you may find that you no longer need bottled sauce.

BAKING

Salt helps to control the activity of yeast, acting as a retardant, thus raising agents will be high in salt. If you use a lot of raising agents, try substituting eggs. It will do the job just as well – and with more flavour.

Avoid self-raising flours as they all have built-in raising agents.

Use salt substitutes or low-sodium salts instead of common salt.

HERBS AND SPICES

Herbs and spices give different, subtle and unusual flavours to many dishes. You can use them fresh – you can even grow them on the kitchen windowsill – or dried. Fresh are nicer in raw, salad-type dishes but dried are fine for cooked dishes. Do make sure, however, that dried herbs are not too old, and keep them in an airtight, dark container, as both air and light will make them go stale more quickly. Dried herbs are a good deal stronger than fresh ones, so do not overdo

Below: When baking, cut down on raising agents, which can contain high levels of salt, by substituting a fine, fresh egg.

when using them for your flavouring. You can use both herbs and spices singly or in combinations. The following list is a guide only; you will need to experiment to find out the combinations that you like best.

- Basil, oregano and marjoram are all excellent both fresh and dried for salads and any casserole dish, especially Italian dishes.
- Mint is lovely fresh and adds greatly to salads.
- Dill weed and caraway seeds are also strong-flavoured and are very popular in northern European cooking – excellent with cabbage and fish dishes.
- Parsley – whether the usual curly variety or the flat-leafed French – has a deliciously robust flavour either cooked or raw. Parsley can be added to almost anything, and it is useful not only for flavour but also for colour and garnishes.

Above: Fresh and dried herbs can be used singly or combined to bring flavour to many savoury dishes.

- Thyme, rosemary, sage and bay leaf, either fresh or dried, are excellent with lamb or pork or in any casserole dish – they are a bit woody to eat uncooked but give very good flavours cooked. You can combine the thyme and bay leaf; the others are probably better on their own.
- Fennel, like coriander, has a distinct flavour of its own, which people either love or hate. It is reminiscent of aniseed and is an excellent herb to use with fish.
- Coriander (both leaf and seed) has become very popular recently and has a wonderful, fresh flavour – although not everyone likes it. Use the fresh leaf in salads, and the seeds or the dried leaf in casseroles or baked dishes.

- Garlic and chives are wonderful flavourings. Garlic can be raw or cooked – boiled, baked in roasts (cut a slit in the roast and insert a peeled clove of garlic), fried or steamed with other vegetables.
- Mustard seeds and horseradish roots are normally found in ready-prepared condiments, but there is no reason why you should not use them raw. Just be careful as both are pretty strong. Peel and grate only the amount needed of fresh horseradish and use in rich, rather fatty foods.
- Salad herbs, such as rocket, sorrel and dandelion, and the more exotic varieties of lettuce like radicchio are now much easier to obtain, and all have delicious flavours of their own.
- Dried seaweeds are now quite easy to obtain. They are very flavoursome and actually taste "salty", although they contain relatively low amounts of sodium.
- Cumin, turmeric and saffron, all north African spices, are delicious with rice and lamb dishes.

- Ginger, both fresh and dried, is a hugely useful spice. It will give a lift to meats and most vegetables.
- Black and green peppercorns – whole or ground – add excellent flavour to almost any dish.

Above: With skilful use of spices and flavourings in your cooking, you will find that you do not miss salt.

- Cinnamon, nutmeg and cloves, although normally used with sweet dishes, work very well in dark meat casseroles and stews and in some lighter dishes too.
- Chilli peppers – from the mild Hungarian paprika to the sizzling Caribbean hot peppers, choose from a delicious range of flavours.

FRUITS

- Lemons – either the juice or rind or both – are invaluable for adding flavour to sweet and savoury dishes.
- Limes look pretty and have a stronger flavour than lemons.
- Oranges, apples, pears and almost any other fruit can also be used successfully in many savoury and sweet dishes to give fresh and interesting flavours. They also look wonderful as garnishes.

Left: Fruits, particularly the citrus kind, are an excellent way of adding fresh and interesting flavour to both sweet and savoury recipes.

OLIVES, CAPERS, NUTS AND SEEDS

These all add variety to dishes in terms of both taste and texture, but there are some things you must bear in mind if you are not to add to the salt content of your food. Make sure, for example, that olives have not been preserved in brine, i.e. salted water.

Make sure, too, that nuts and seeds are not the salted variety. Add flavour to nuts (peanuts, cashews, almonds,

walnuts, Brazils, etc.) and seeds (pumpkin, sunflower, sesame, pomegranate, etc.) by browning them, without fat, in a frying pan or an oven or under a grill.

Above and above left: Nuts, seeds, capers and olives will give a boost to texture and flavour, but be sure to buy them unsalted. Use dried seaweeds for their "salty" flavour and dried chillies for their zing.

REDUCED-SODIUM SALTS

There are now several reduced-sodium salts on the market. Some are available in supermarkets and some are more likely to be found in delicatessens and health-food stores. They include:

• **LoSalt** – a reduced-sodium "salt", which contains only 13.22 per cent sodium per gram of salt instead of the normal 40 per cent.
• **Solo** – a low-sodium natural sea salt from Iceland which contains 16.28 per cent sodium.
• **Ruthmol** – a potassium salt consisting of less than 1 per cent sodium and 23.8 per cent potassium.
• **Seagreens** – an organic seaweed from the Arctic, ground into powder, which contains 3.5 per cent sodium, 2.5 per cent potassium and a whole range of other beneficial nutrients.

Although none of these tastes quite the same as a traditional sea salt when you taste them by themselves, they are quite acceptable when they are used in cooking and can even fool some salt enthusiasts.

Above: Reduced-sodium salts and (front) Seagreens, an organic seaweed, which contains a range of nutrients as well as adding flavour.

MENU PLANNING

Many people think that to eat healthily signifies the end of exciting meals, and entertaining and eating out will be a thing of the past.

A little planning, however, can ensure entertaining at home that is varied, delicious and low in salt. Below are some menu hints to get you started.

Spicy and Aromatic
Chilled Vegetable Soup with Pastis
Aromatic Chicken
Roasted Root Vegetables with
　whole spices

Light Dining
Creamy Aubergine Dip
Tuna with Garlic, Tomatoes and
　Herbs, served with fried potatoes
Couscous Salad

Hearty Winter Fare
Wild Mushroom Soup
Roast Leg of Lamb with Vegetables,
　such as carrots, potatoes and broccoli
Irish Whiskey Cake

Combining Colour and Texture
Calamari with Double Tomato
  Stuffing and Pane Toscana
Beef Tagine with Sweet Potatoes
Provencale Vegetable Stew

A Vegetarian's Delight
Spiced Coconut Mushrooms
Vegetarian Fried Noodles
Sweet-and-sour Artichoke Salad with
  salsa agrodolce

EATING OUT

Although some restaurants are very helpful and will give you detailed ingredients lists for their dishes, there is no legal requirement on them to do so. Even if they can give you ingredients lists, it is unlikely that they will have very much idea of how much salt/ sodium those dishes contain, especially if they are not wholly made on the premises, as so many restaurant dishes are.

Once again, if your salt intake is not critical, you should use the "high salt" list given earlier and avoid any of the dishes on it. If you keep your choices to simple dishes such as roasts and plainly cooked vegetables dressed with a little oil or butter and fresh fruits or fruit salads for dessert, you should be OK. If your salt intake is critical, you should speak to the restaurant in advance, explain to them that you are on a no-salt/very low-salt diet and ask them if they can prepare something specially for you that does not use salt.

The same applies if you are eating out with friends or relatives. Call them in plenty of time, and warn them that you are on a very low-salt diet.

TRYING NEW CUISINES

Many non-Western cuisines rely far less on salt as a flavouring than we do. It is therefore worth experimenting with other cuisines – even if you do not adopt them wholesale. Mediterranean cooking uses rich vegetables and oils to give deep and exciting flavours. Thai and Indonesian foods are full of herbs and spices, while Mexican and South American cooking use the many flavours of the chilli and the tomato families to add taste to foods.

SOUPS AND STARTERS

Though the prelude to a meal, soups and starters should shine in their own right. Hearty and wholesome or quick and light, the following recipes explore a wide range of ingredients and flavours, from baby squid to saffron strands, each recipe showing just how easy it is to make delicious, flavoursome food without recourse to salt. Choose from dishes such as Wild Mushroom Soup, Grilled Vegetable Terrine, Calamari with Double Tomato Stuffing and Creamy Aubergine Dip.

Wild Mushroom Soup

Wild mushrooms can sometimes be expensive but dried porcini have an intense flavour, so only a small quantity is needed. The beef stock may seem unusual in a vegetable soup, but it helps to strengthen the earthy flavour of the mushrooms.

INGREDIENTS

Serves 4

25g/1oz/2 cups dried porcini mushrooms
30ml/2 tbsp olive oil
15g/½oz/1 tbsp unsalted butter
2 leeks, finely sliced
2 shallots, roughly chopped
1 garlic clove, roughly chopped
225g/8oz/3 cups fresh wild mushrooms
about 1.2 litres/2 pints/5 cups hot home-made beef stock
2.5ml/½ tsp dried thyme
150ml/¼ pint/⅔ cup double cream
freshly ground black pepper, to taste
fresh thyme sprigs, to garnish

1 Put the porcini in a bowl, add 250ml/8fl oz/1 cup warm water and leave to soak for 20–30 minutes. Lift the porcini out of the liquid and squeeze over the bowl to remove as much of the soaking liquid as possible. Strain all the liquid and reserve to use later. Finely chop the porcini.

2 Heat the oil and butter in a large saucepan until foaming. Add the sliced leeks, chopped shallots and garlic, and cook gently for about 5 minutes, stirring frequently, until softened but not coloured.

3 Chop or slice the fresh mushrooms and add to the pan. Stir over a medium heat for a few minutes until they begin to soften. Pour in the stock and bring to the boil. Add the porcini, soaking liquid, dried thyme and pepper to taste. Lower the heat, half-cover the pan and simmer gently for 30 minutes, stirring occasionally.

4 Pour about three-quarters of the soup into a food processor or blender, and process until smooth. Return to the soup remaining in the pan, stir in the cream and heat through. Taste for seasoning. Serve garnished with thyme sprigs.

NUTRITION NOTES	
Per portion:	
Energy	296Kcals/1223kJ
Protein	4.8g
Fat	27.3g
Saturated fat	14.09g
Carbohydrate	8g
Fibre	1.9g
Sodium	50mg

Spicy Lamb Soup

This spicy, filling soup, based on a traditional Moroccan recipe, combines pulses with lamb and fresh tomatoes.

INGREDIENTS

Serves 6

75g/3oz/½ cup chick-peas,
  soaked overnight
15g/½oz/1 tbsp unsalted butter
225g/8oz lamb, cubed
1 onion, chopped
450g/1lb tomatoes, chopped
a few celery leaves, chopped
30ml/2 tbsp chopped fresh parsley
15ml/1 tbsp chopped fresh coriander
2.5ml/½ tsp ground ginger
2.5ml/½ tsp ground turmeric
5ml/1 tsp ground cinnamon
75g/3oz/scant ½ cup green lentils
75g/3oz vermicelli or soup pasta
2 egg yolks
juice of ½–1 lemon
freshly ground black pepper
fresh coriander, to garnish
lemon wedges, to serve

1 Drain the chick-peas, rinse under cold water and set aside. Melt the butter in a large, flameproof casserole or saucepan and fry the lamb and onion for 2–3 minutes, stirring, until the lamb is just browned.

2 Add the tomatoes, celery leaves, herbs and spices, and season well with black pepper. Cook for about 1 minute and then stir in 1.75 litres/ 3 pints/7½ cups water and add the lentils and chick-peas.

3 Slowly bring to the boil and skim the surface to remove the surplus froth. Boil rapidly for 10 minutes, then reduce the heat and simmer very gently for about 2 hours or until the chick-peas are tender. Season with a little more pepper if necessary.

4 Add the vermicelli or soup pasta and cook for 5–6 minutes until it is just cooked through.

NUTRITION NOTES	
Per portion:	
Energy	256Kcals/1074kJ
Protein	16.3g
Fat	10g
Saturated fat	4.51g
Carbohydrate	27g
Fibre	4.1g
Sodium	41mg

5 If the soup is very thick at this stage, add a little more water. Beat the egg yolks with the lemon juice and stir into the simmering soup.

6 Immediately remove the soup from the heat and stir until thickened. Pour into warmed serving bowls and garnish with the fresh coriander. Serve with lemon wedges.

Chilled Vegetable Soup with Pastis

Fennel, star anise and pastis give a delicate aniseed flavour to this sophisticated soup.

INGREDIENTS

Serves 6

175g/6oz leeks, finely sliced
225g/8oz fennel, finely sliced
1 potato, peeled and diced
3 pieces star anise, tied in a square of muslin
300ml/½ pint/1¼ cups single cream
10ml/2 tsp pastis
90ml/6 tbsp double cream or crème fraîche
freshly ground black pepper
snipped chives, to garnish

COOK'S TIP

To chill the soup quickly, stir in a spoonful of crushed ice.

1 Pour 900ml/1½ pints/3¾ cups boiling water into a saucepan, add the sliced leek and fennel, the diced potato and star anise and season to taste with pepper. Bring to the boil and simmer for 25 minutes.

2 Remove the star anise with a slotted spoon, then process the vegetables until smooth in a food processor or blender and place in a clean pan.

3 Stir in the single cream, bring to the boil, taste and adjust the seasoning if necessary.

4 Strain through a sieve into a bowl, cover and leave until cold. To serve, stir in the pastis, pour into individual serving bowls, add a swirl of double cream or a spoonful of crème fraîche and garnish with snipped chives.

NUTRITION NOTES

Per portion:

Energy	194Kcals/801kJ
Protein	2.7g
Fat	17g
Saturated fat	10.51g
Carbohydrate	7g
Fibre	1.8g
Sodium	36mg

Mediterranean Fish Soup

This traditional soup is a delight for lovers of herbs and is perfect when topped off with a dollop of garlic mayonnaise. Use as many varieties of fish and shellfish as you can find.

INGREDIENTS

Serves 4

450g/1lb mixed fish fillets, such as
   red mullet, monkfish, sea bass
450g/1lb mixed shellfish, such as
   mussels and prawns
a pinch of saffron strands
60ml/4 tbsp olive oil
350g/12oz onions,
   roughly chopped
350g/12oz fennel, halved and thinly
   sliced (about 1 small bulb)
10ml/2 tsp plain flour
400g/14oz can chopped tomatoes
3 garlic cloves, crushed
2 bay leaves
30ml/2 tbsp chopped fresh thyme
pared rind of 1 orange
cayenne pepper, to taste
saltless garlic mayonnaise and crusty
   bread, to serve

1 Wash and skin the fish, if necessary, and cut into large chunks. Clean the shellfish and remove the heads from the prawns. Discard any mussels that are open.

2 Place the saffron strands in a bowl and pour over 150ml/¼ pint/⅔ cup boiling water. Leave the saffron to soak for about 20 minutes. Strain.

3 Heat the oil in a large saucepan and add the onions and fennel. Fry for 5 minutes, stirring occasionally with a wooden spoon, or until they are beginning to soften. Stir in the flour.

4 Strain the tomatoes and gradually blend in with 750ml/1¼ pints/3 cups cold water, the garlic, bay leaves, thyme, orange rind, saffron liquid and cayenne pepper. Bring to the boil.

5 Reduce the heat, add the fish (not the shellfish) and simmer gently, uncovered, for about 2 minutes.

6 Add the shellfish and cook for a further 2–3 minutes, or until all the fish is cooked but still holding its shape. Discard any mussels that haven't opened. Adjust the seasoning to taste. Serve with a generous spoonful of garlic mayonnaise and crusty bread.

NUTRITION NOTES	
Per portion:	
Energy	340Kcals/1412kJ
Protein	29.7g
Fat	18.6g
Saturated fat	3.3g
Carbohydrate	14g
Fibre	3.6g
Sodium	205mg

Grilled Vegetable Terrine

This is a colourful layered terrine, using all the vegetables evocative of the Mediterranean, with an added richness from the red wine vinegar.

INGREDIENTS

Serves 6
2 large red peppers, quartered, cored and seeded
2 large yellow peppers, quartered, cored and seeded
1 large aubergine, sliced lengthways
2 large courgettes, sliced lengthways
90ml/6 tbsp olive oil
1 large red onion, finely sliced
75g/3oz/½ cup raisins
15ml/1 tbsp red wine vinegar
400ml/14fl oz/1⅔ cups tomato juice
15g/½oz/2 tbsp powdered gelatine
fresh basil leaves, to garnish

For the dressing
90ml/6 tbsp extra virgin olive oil
30ml/2 tbsp red wine vinegar
freshly ground black pepper

1 Place the prepared peppers skin-side up under a hot grill and cook until the skins are blackened. Transfer to a bowl and cover. Leave to cool.

2 Arrange the aubergine and courgette slices on separate baking sheets. Brush them with a little olive oil and cook under the grill, turning occasionally, until tender and golden.

3 Heat the remaining oil in a frying pan and add the sliced onion, raisins and red wine vinegar. Cook gently until soft and syrupy. Leave to cool in the frying pan.

4 Lightly grease a 1.75 litre/3 pint/7½ cup terrine with oil and then line with clear film, leaving a little hanging over the sides.

5 Pour half the tomato juice into a saucepan and sprinkle with the gelatine. Dissolve gently over a low heat, stirring.

6 Skin and slice the cooled peppers. Place a layer of red peppers in the bottom of the terrine and pour in enough of the tomato juice and gelatine mixture to cover. Next add a layer of aubergine and pour over enough tomato juice to cover.

7 Continue building layers with the courgettes, yellow peppers and onion mixture, finishing with a last layer of red peppers. Pour tomato juice over each layer of vegetables as you go.

8 Add the remaining tomato juice to any left in the pan and pour into the terrine. Give it a sharp tap to disperse the juice. Cover the terrine and chill until set.

9 To make the dressing, whisk together the oil and vinegar and season with pepper. Turn out the terrine and remove the clear film. Serve in thick slices, drizzled with the dressing. Garnish with basil leaves.

NUTRITION NOTES	
Per portion:	
Energy	319Kcals/1322kJ
Protein	6.3g
Fat	23g
Saturated fat	3.18g
Carbohydrate	23g
Fibre	5.1g
Sodium	170mg

Chicken Goujons

Herbs and spices ensure these
chicken pieces are full of flavour.

INGREDIENTS

Serves 8

4 boned and skinned
  chicken breasts
175g/6oz/3 cups fresh
  saltless breadcrumbs
5ml/1 tsp ground coriander
10ml/2 tsp ground paprika
2.5ml/½ tsp ground cumin
45g/1¼ oz/3 tbsp plain flour
2 eggs, beaten
vegetable oil, for deep-frying
freshly ground black pepper
lemon wedges and fresh coriander
  sprigs, to garnish

For the dip

275g/10oz/1¼ cups plain yogurt
30ml/2 tbsp lemon juice
60ml/4 tbsp chopped fresh coriander
60ml/4 tbsp chopped fresh parsley

1 Divide each chicken breast into
two fillets. Place them between
two sheets of clear film and, using a
rolling pin, flatten each one to a
thickness of about 5mm/¼in.

2 Cut diagonally across the fillets to
form 2.5cm/1in strips.

3 Mix the breadcrumbs with the
spices and seasoning. Toss the
chicken fillet pieces in the flour,
keeping them separate.

4 Dip the fillets into the beaten egg
and then coat in the breadcrumbs.

5 Thoroughly mix together all the
ingredients for the dip and season
with pepper to taste. Cover and chill
until required.

6 Heat the oil in a heavy-based pan.
It is ready for deep-frying when a
cube of bread tossed into the oil sizzles
on the surface. Fry the goujons in
batches until golden and crisp. Drain
on kitchen paper and keep warm in
the oven until all the goujons have
been fried. Garnish with lemon
wedges and fresh coriander before
serving with the dip.

NUTRITION NOTES	
Per portion:	
Energy	555Kcals/2334kJ
Protein	49.1g
Fat	19.2g
Saturated fat	3.2g
Carbohydrate	50g
Fibre	1.8g
Sodium	536mg

Calamari with Double Tomato Stuffing

Calamari, or baby squid, should be cooked only briefly – just until they turn opaque – or they will become tough and rubbery. Turn and baste them often.

INGREDIENTS

Serves 4

500g/1¼lb baby squid, cleaned
1 garlic clove, crushed
3 plum tomatoes, skinned and chopped
8 sun-dried tomatoes in oil, drained and chopped
60ml/4 tbsp chopped fresh basil, plus extra, to serve
60ml/4 tbsp fresh saltless white breadcrumbs
45ml/3 tbsp olive oil
15ml/1 tbsp red wine vinegar
freshly ground black pepper
lemon wedges, to serve

1 Remove the tentacles from the squid and roughly chop them. Leave the body of the squid whole.

2 Mix together the squid tentacles, garlic, plum tomatoes, sun-dried tomatoes, basil and breadcrumbs. Stir in 15ml/1 tbsp of the oil and the vinegar. Season well with pepper.

3 Soak some wooden cocktail sticks in water for 10 minutes before use, to prevent them burning.

4 Fill the squid with the stuffing mixture using a teaspoon: do not overstuff. Secure the open ends with the soaked cocktail sticks.

5 Brush the squid with the remaining oil and cook over a medium-hot barbecue or under a preheated grill for 4–5 minutes, turning often. Sprinkle with basil and serve with lemon wedges.

NUTRITION NOTES	
Per portion:	
Energy	238Kcals/995kJ
Protein	21.8g
Fat	11.4g
Saturated fat	1.38g
Carbohydrate	13g
Fibre	1.8g
Sodium	484mg

Skewered Lamb with Red Onion Salsa

This tapas dish can be cooked under a conventional grill or outdoors on the barbecue on warm summer nights. The simple, tangy salsa makes a refreshing accompaniment – you will get best results if you use a mild-flavoured red onion that is fresh and crisp, and a tomato that is ripe and full of flavour.

INGREDIENTS

Serves 4
225g/8oz lean lamb
2.5ml/½ tsp ground cumin
5ml/1 tsp ground paprika
15ml/1 tbsp olive oil
freshly ground black pepper

For the red onion salsa
1 red onion, finely sliced
1 large tomato, seeded
  and chopped
15ml/1 tbsp red wine vinegar
3–4 fresh basil or mint leaves,
  roughly torn
small mint leaves, to garnish

1 Using a sharp knife, chop the lamb into cubes. Place the cubes in a bowl with the cumin, paprika, olive oil and plenty of pepper. Toss well until the lamb is coated with the spices.

2 Cover the bowl with clear film and leave in a cool place for several hours, or in the fridge overnight if possible, so that the lamb absorbs the spicy flavours.

3 When ready to use, spread the lamb cubes on four small skewers – if using wooden skewers, soak them first in cold water for at least 30 minutes to prevent them from burning during cooking.

4 To make the salsa, put the sliced onion, tomato, vinegar and basil or mint leaves in a small bowl and stir together until thoroughly blended. Season to taste with pepper, garnish with mint, then set aside while you cook the skewered lamb.

5 Cook the lamb under a preheated grill or over a hot barbecue for about 5–10 minutes, turning the skewers frequently, until the lamb is well browned but still slightly pink in the centre. Serve hot with the onion salsa, garnished with mint leaves.

COOK'S TIP

To chill the soup quickly, stir in a spoonful of crushed ice.

NUTRITION NOTES

Per portion:
Energy	136Kcals/568kJ
Protein	12.3g
Fat	7.9g
Saturated fat	2.77g
Carbohydrate	4g
Fibre	0.8g
Sodium	56mg

Creamy Aubergine Dip

Spread this velvet-textured aubergine dip thickly on toasted rounds of low-salt bread, then top them with slivers of sun-dried tomato to make wonderful, Italian-style crostini.

INGREDIENTS

Serves 4

1 large aubergine
30ml/2 tbsp olive oil
1 small onion, finely chopped
2 garlic cloves, finely chopped
30ml/2 tbsp chopped fresh parsley
75ml/5 tbsp crème fraîche
Tabasco sauce, to taste
juice of 1 lemon
freshly ground black pepper
toasted rounds of saltless bread and
    sun-dried tomato slivers, to serve

1 Preheat the grill. Place the whole aubergine on a baking sheet and grill it for 2–3 minutes, turning occasionally, until the skin is blackened and wrinkled and the aubergine feels soft when squeezed.

2 Cover the aubergine with a clean dish towel and allow to cool for about 5 minutes.

3 Heat the oil in a frying pan and cook the onion and garlic for 5 minutes until softened but not browned.

4 Peel the skin from the aubergine. Mash the flesh with a large fork or potato masher to make a pulpy purée.

5 Stir in the onion, garlic, parsley and crème fraîche. Add the Tabasco sauce, lemon juice and pepper to taste. Transfer the dip to a serving bowl and serve warm, or allow to cool and serve at room temperature, accompanied by slices of toasted bread and slivers of sun-dried tomato.

NUTRITION NOTES	
Per portion:	
Energy	147Kcals/610kJ
Protein	1.9g
Fat	13.5g
Saturated fat	5.46g
Carbohydrate	5g
Fibre	2.6g
Sodium	12mg

Mellow Garlic Dip

Two whole heads of garlic may seem like a lot but, once cooked, they develop a sweet and mellow flavour. Serve with crunchy home-made low-salt bread sticks and crudités.

INGREDIENTS

Serves 4
2 whole garlic heads
15ml/1 tbsp olive oil
60ml/4 tbsp saltless mayonnaise
75ml/5 tbsp Greek yogurt
5ml/1 tsp wholegrain mustard
freshly ground black pepper
low-salt breadsticks, to serve

1 Preheat the oven to 200°C/400°F/ Gas 6. Separate the garlic cloves and place them, unpeeled, in a small roasting tin.

2 Pour the olive oil over the garlic cloves and turn them with a spoon to coat them evenly. Roast for 20–30 minutes until the garlic is tender and softened. Leave to cool for 5 minutes.

3 Trim off the root end of each roasted garlic clove. Peel the cloves and discard the skins.

5 Place the garlic in a small bowl and stir in the mayonnaise, yogurt and wholegrain mustard.

NUTRITION NOTES	
Per portion:	
Energy	175Kcals/720kJ
Protein	1.6g
Fat	18.6g
Saturated fat	3.17g
Carbohydrate	0g
Fibre	0.1g
Sodium	40mg

4 Place the roasted garlic cloves on a chopping board and mash with a fork until puréed.

6 Spoon the dip into a serving bowl and season to taste with pepper. Serve accompanied by breadsticks.

SALADS AND VEGETABLE ACCOMPANIMENTS

Whether salads and vegetables are part of a vegetarian meal or the accompaniment to a meat or fish dish, there is no reason why they shouldn't be full of flavour and interest. But it can be difficult to know where to start. The recipes included here, however, such as Sweet-and-sour Artichoke Salad and Spiced Coconut Mushrooms, will give you plenty of wonderful ideas.

Sweet-and-sour Artichoke Salad

Agrodolce is a sweet-and-sour sauce, which works perfectly in this artichoke salad.

INGREDIENTS

Serves 4–6
6 small globe artichokes
juice of 1 lemon
30ml/2 tbsp olive oil
2 medium onions, roughly chopped
175g/6oz/1 cup fresh or frozen broad
  beans (shelled weight)
175g/6oz/1½ cups fresh or frozen peas
  (shelled weight)
freshly ground black pepper
fresh mint leaves, to garnish

For the salsa agrodolce
120ml/4fl oz/½ cup white
  wine vinegar
15ml/1 tbsp caster sugar
a handful of fresh mint leaves,
  roughly torn

1 Peel the outer leaves from the artichokes and discard. Cut the artichokes into quarters and place in a bowl of water with the lemon juice.

2 Heat the oil in a large saucepan and add the onions. Cook until the onions are golden. Add the beans and stir, then drain the artichokes and add to the pan. Pour in about 300ml/½ pint/1¼ cups water and cook, covered, for 10–15 minutes.

3 Add the peas, season with pepper and cook for a further 5 minutes, stirring from time to time, until the vegetables are tender. Strain through a sieve and place all the vegetables in a bowl. Leave to cool, then chill.

4 To make the salsa agrodolce, mix together all the ingredients in a small pan. Heat gently for 2–3 minutes until the sugar has dissolved. Simmer gently for about 5 minutes, stirring occasionally. Leave to cool. To serve, drizzle the salsa over the vegetables and garnish with mint leaves.

NUTRITION NOTES	
Per portion:	
Energy	162Kcals/678kJ
Protein	8.2g
Fat	6.6g
Saturated fat	0.96g
Carbohydrate	19g
Fibre	5.7g
Sodium	31mg

Couscous Salad

Couscous salad is popular almost everywhere nowadays. This salad has a delicate flavour and is excellent served with grilled chicken or kebabs.

INGREDIENTS

Serves 4

275g/10oz/1⅔ cups couscous
550ml/18fl oz/2½ cups boiling home-
  made vegetable stock
12 black olives in oil
2 small courgettes
25g/1oz/¼ cup flaked almonds,
  toasted
60ml/4 tbsp olive oil
15ml/1 tbsp lemon juice
15ml/1 tbsp chopped fresh coriander
15ml/1 tbsp chopped fresh parsley
a good pinch of ground cumin
a good pinch of cayenne pepper

1 Place the couscous in a large bowl and pour over the boiling stock. Stir with a fork, and then set aside for about 10 minutes for the stock to be absorbed. Fluff up with a fork.

NUTRITION NOTES	
Per portion:	
Energy	341Kcals/1418kJ
Protein	7g
Fat	19.2g
Saturated fat	2.5g
Carbohydrate	37g
Fibre	1.4g
Sodium	354mg

2 Drain the olives and halve them, discarding the stones. Top and tail the courgettes and cut into small julienne strips.

3 Carefully mix the courgettes, olives and almonds into the couscous.

4 Blend together the olive oil, lemon juice, herbs and spices, and stir into the salad. Serve at room temperature.

COOK'S TIP
If you prefer, you can reconstitute the pre-cooked couscous by steaming it.

Orange and Red Onion Salad with Cumin

Cumin and mint give this lovely summer salad a Middle Eastern flavour. Choose small, seedless oranges if you can.

INGREDIENTS

Serves 6
6 oranges
2 red onions, finely sliced
15ml/1 tbsp cumin seeds
5ml/1 tsp freshly ground
   black pepper
15ml/1 tbsp chopped fresh mint
90ml/6 tbsp olive oil
fresh mint sprigs and black olives
   in oil, to serve

COOK'S TIP

It is important to let the salad stand for 2 hours, so that the flavours develop and the onion softens slightly, but do not leave the salad for much longer than this.

---

1 Slice the oranges thinly, working over a bowl to catch any juice. Then, holding each orange slice in turn over the bowl, cut round with scissors to remove the peel and pith. Separate the onion slices into rings.

2 Arrange the orange slices and onion rings in layers in a shallow dish, sprinkling each layer with cumin seeds, black pepper, mint and olive oil. Pour over the orange juice saved while slicing the oranges. Leave the salad to marinate for about 2 hours.

3 Just before serving, scatter the salad with the fresh sprigs of mint and drained black olives.

NUTRITION NOTES

Per portion:	
Energy	178Kcals/740kJ
Protein	2.6g
Fat	11.6g
Saturated fat	1.56g
Carbohydrate	17g
Fibre	3.1g
Sodium	12mg

Spanish Salad with Capers and Olives

Sweet, ripe tomatoes are the perfect foil to the sharp tang of capers and olives.

INGREDIENTS

Serves 4
4 tomatoes, peeled and finely diced
½ cucumber, peeled and finely diced
1 bunch spring onions
1 bunch purslane or watercress, washed
8 pimiento-stuffed olives in oil
15ml/1 tbsp capers in vinegar, drained

For the dressing
30ml/2 tbsp red wine vinegar
5ml/1 tsp paprika
2.5ml/½ tsp ground cumin
1 garlic clove, crushed
75ml/5 tbsp olive oil
freshly ground black pepper

1 Put the tomatoes and cucumber in a bowl. Trim and chop half the spring onions, add them to the salad bowl and mix lightly.

2 Break the purslane or watercress into small sprigs. Add to the tomato mixture, along with the olives and capers.

NUTRITION NOTES

Per portion:	
Energy	185Kcals/765kJ
Protein	2.7g
Fat	17.3g
Saturated fat	2.4g
Carbohydrate	5g
Fibre	2.4g
Sodium	330mg

3 Make the dressing. Mix the wine vinegar, paprika, cumin and garlic in a bowl. Whisk in the oil and add pepper to taste. Pour over the salad and toss lightly. Serve with the remaining trimmed spring onions.

Courgettes Italian-style

The olive oil gives this dish a delicious fragrance but does not overpower the courgettes.

INGREDIENTS

Serves 4

15ml/1 tbsp olive oil
15ml/1 tbsp sunflower oil
1 large onion, chopped
1 garlic clove, crushed
4–5 medium courgettes, sliced
150ml/¼ pint/⅔ cup hot home-made
    chicken or vegetable stock
2.5ml/½ tsp chopped fresh oregano
freshly ground black pepper
chopped fresh parsley, to garnish

1 Heat the oils in a large frying pan and fry the onion and garlic over a moderate heat for 5–6 minutes until the onion has softened and is beginning to brown.

2 Add the courgettes slices and fry for about 4 minutes until they just begin to be flecked with brown on both sides. Stir frequently.

3 Stir in the stock, fresh oregano and pepper, and simmer gently for about 8–10 minutes until the liquid has almost evaporated. Spoon the courgettes into a serving dish, sprinkle with chopped fresh parsley and serve.

NUTRITION NOTES

Per portion:	
Energy	82Kcals/338kJ
Protein	2.2g
Fat	5.9g
Saturated fat	0.84g
Carbohydrate	5g
Fibre	1.4g
Sodium	6mg

Potato, Broccoli and Red Pepper Stir-fry

A hot and hearty stir-fry of vegetables, with just a hint of piquancy from the fresh ginger and groundnut oil.

INGREDIENTS

Serves 2
450g/1lb potatoes
45ml/3 tbsp groundnut oil
50g/2oz/¼ cup unsalted butter
1 small onion, chopped
1 red pepper, seeded and chopped
225g/8oz broccoli, broken
　　into florets
2.5cm/1in piece fresh root ginger,
　　peeled and grated
freshly ground black pepper

1 Peel the potatoes and cut them into 1cm/½in cubes.

2 Heat the oil in a large frying pan and add the potatoes. Cook for 8 minutes over a high heat, stirring and tossing occasionally, until the potatoes are browned and just tender.

3 Drain off the oil. Add the butter to the potatoes in the pan. As soon as it melts, add the onion and red pepper. Stir-fry for 2 minutes.

4 Add the broccoli florets and ginger to the pan. Stir-fry for 2–3 minutes more, taking care not to break up the potatoes. Add plenty of pepper to taste and serve at once.

NUTRITION NOTES

Per portion:
Energy	579Kcals/2421kJ
Protein	11.1g
Fat	38.9g
Saturated fat	16.18g
Carbohydrate	49g
Fibre	7.6g
Sodium	31mg

COOK'S TIP

Although a wok is the preferred pan for stir-frying, for this recipe a flat frying pan is best to cook the potatoes quickly.

Glazed Sweet Potatoes with Ginger and Allspice

Fried sweet potatoes acquire a candied coating when cooked with ginger syrup and allspice, while the cayenne pepper adds a touch of zing.

INGREDIENTS

Serves 4
900g/2lb sweet potatoes
50g/2oz/¼ cup unsalted butter
45ml/3 tbsp oil
2 garlic cloves, crushed
2 pieces stem ginger, finely chopped
10ml/2 tsp ground allspice
15ml/1 tbsp syrup from ginger jar
cayenne pepper, to taste
10ml/2 tsp chopped fresh thyme,
   plus a few sprigs to garnish

1 Peel the sweet potatoes and cut into 1cm/½in cubes. Melt the butter with the oil in a large frying pan. Add the sweet potato cubes and fry, stirring frequently, for about 10 minutes until they are just soft.

2 Stir in the garlic, ginger and ground allspice. Cook, stirring occasionally, for 5 minutes more. Stir in the ginger syrup, a generous pinch of cayenne pepper and the chopped thyme. Stir for 1–2 minutes more, then serve in warmed bowls scattered with fresh thyme sprigs.

--- NUTRITION NOTES ---

Per portion:	
Energy	359Kcals/1499kJ
Protein	2.7g
Fat	19.3g
Saturated fat	7.75g
Carbohydrate	47g
Fibre	4.7g
Sodium	89mg

Roasted Root Vegetables with Whole Spices

The beauty of roast vegetables is that they virtually cook themselves. Adding a few well-chosen herbs and spices is the only touch required.

INGREDIENTS

Serves 4
3 parsnips, peeled
3 potatoes, peeled
3 carrots, peeled
3 sweet potatoes, peeled
60ml/4 tbsp olive oil
8 shallots, peeled
2 garlic cloves, sliced
10ml/2 tsp white mustard seeds
10ml/2 tsp coriander seeds,
   lightly crushed
5ml/1 tsp cumin seeds
2 bay leaves
freshly ground black pepper

1 Preheat the oven to 190°C/375°F/ Gas 5. Bring a saucepan of water to the boil. Cut the parsnips, potatoes, carrots and sweet potatoes into chunks. Add them to the pan and bring the water back to the boil. Boil for 2 minutes, then drain.

2 Pour the olive oil into a large, heavy roasting tin and place over a moderate heat. Add the vegetables, shallots and garlic. Fry, tossing the vegetables over the heat until they are pale golden at the edges.

3 Add the mustard seeds, coriander seeds, cumin seeds and bay leaves. Cook for 1 minute, then season with pepper. Transfer the roasting tin to the oven and roast for 45 minutes, turning occasionally, until the vegetables are crisp and golden and cooked through.

--- NUTRITION NOTES ---

Per portion:	
Energy	373Kcals/1559kJ
Protein	7.2g
Fat	14.2g
Saturated fat	1.71g
Carbohydrate	58g
Fibre	10.1g
Sodium	80mg

--- VARIATION ---

Vary the selection of vegetables according to what is available. Try using swede or pumpkin instead of, or as well as, the vegetables suggested.

Stuffed Tomatoes and Peppers

Colourful peppers and tomatoes make perfect containers for various meat and vegetable stuffings. This rice and herb version uses typically Greek ingredients.

INGREDIENTS

Serves 4

2 large ripe tomatoes
1 green pepper
1 yellow or orange pepper
60ml/4 tbsp olive oil, plus extra for sprinkling
2 onions, chopped
2 garlic cloves, crushed
50g/2oz/½ cup blanched almonds, chopped
75g/3oz/scant ½ cup long-grain rice, boiled and drained
15g/½oz fresh mint, roughly chopped
15g/½oz fresh parsley, chopped
25g/1oz/2 tbsp sultanas
45ml/3 tbsp ground almonds
freshly ground black pepper
chopped fresh herbs, to garnish

1 Preheat the oven to 190°C/375°F/ Gas 5. Cut the tomatoes in half and scoop out the insides. Drain the halves and roughly chop the insides.

2 Halve the peppers, leaving the cores intact. Scoop out the seeds and white pith. Brush the peppers with 15ml/1 tbsp of the oil and bake on a baking tray for 15 minutes. Place the peppers and tomatoes in an oven-proof dish and season with pepper.

NUTRITION NOTES	
Per portion:	
Energy	340Kcals/1411kJ
Protein	8.1g
Fat	25g
Saturated fat	2.65g
Carbohydrate	22g
Fibre	5.1g
Sodium	19mg

3 Fry the onions in the remaining oil for 5 minutes. Add the garlic and chopped almonds and fry for 1 minute more.

4 Remove the pan from the heat and stir in the rice, chopped tomatoes, mint, parsley and sultanas. Season well with pepper and spoon the mixture into the tomato and pepper halves.

5 Pour 150ml/¼ pint/⅔ cup boiling water around the tomatoes and peppers and bake, uncovered, for 20 minutes. Scatter with the ground almonds and sprinkle with a little extra olive oil. Return to the oven and bake for a further 20 minutes, or until turning golden. Serve garnished with chopped fresh herbs.

Spiced Coconut Mushrooms

Here is a simple and delicious way to cook mushrooms. The use of groundnut oil adds a pleasant, subtle flavour. They may be served with almost any Asian meal as well as with grilled or roasted meats and poultry.

INGREDIENTS

Serves 3–4

10ml/2 tbsp groundnut oil
2 garlic cloves, finely chopped
2 red chillies, seeded and sliced
   into rings
3 shallots, finely chopped
225g/8oz/3 cups button mushrooms,
   thickly sliced
150ml/¼ pint/⅔ cup coconut milk
30ml/2 tbsp finely chopped
   fresh coriander
freshly ground black pepper

1 Heat a wok or frying pan until hot, add the oil and swirl it around, coating the sides of the wok well. When the oil is hot, add the chopped garlic and chillies, then stir-fry for a few seconds.

2 Add the chopped shallots and stir-fry for 2–3 minutes until softened. Add the sliced mushrooms and stir-fry for 3 minutes more.

4 Taste and season as necessary. Sprinkle over the coriander and toss gently to mix. Serve at once.

3 Pour in the coconut milk and bring to the boil. Boil rapidly over high heat until the liquid is reduced by half and coats the mushrooms.

NUTRITION NOTES	
Per portion:	
Energy	95Kcals/394kJ
Protein	2.2g
Fat	7.9g
Saturated fat	1.48g
Carbohydrate	4g
Fibre	1.2g
Sodium	63mg

MAIN MEALS

Using pork, poultry, lamb, beef, fish or vegetables as their main ingredient, these fantastic dishes from all over the world are so rich in texture, colour and flavour that you'll never notice that you didn't rely on the salt cellar. Whether you are after something traditional like Roast Leg of Lamb with Mushroom Stuffing and Irish Stew, or choose to explore the cuisines of the world with dishes such as Beef Tagine with Sweet Potatoes or Spiced Tofu Stir-fry, you'll be delighted with the results.

Paprika Pork with Fennel and Caraway

Fennel always tastes particularly
good with pork, and combined
with caraway seeds adds an
aromatic flavour to this dish.

INGREDIENTS

Serves 4

15ml/1 tbsp olive oil
4 boneless pork steaks
1 large onion, thinly sliced
400g/14oz can chopped tomatoes
5ml/1 tsp fennel seeds, lightly crushed
2.5ml/½ tsp caraway seeds, crushed
15ml/1 tbsp paprika, plus extra
   to garnish
30ml/2 tbsp soured cream
freshly ground black pepper
noodles tossed with poppy seeds,
   to serve

1 Heat the oil in a large frying pan.
Add the pork steaks and brown on
both sides. Lift out the steaks and put
them on a plate.

2 Add the onion to the oil remaining
in the pan. Cook for 10 minutes
until soft and golden.

3 Stir in the tomatoes, fennel seeds,
caraway seeds and paprika.

4 Return the pork to the pan and
simmer gently for 20–30 minutes
until tender. Season with pepper.

5 Lightly swirl in the soured cream
and sprinkle with a little extra
paprika. Serve with noodles that have
been tossed in poppy seeds.

NUTRITION NOTES	
Per portion:	
Energy	254Kcals/1064kJ
Protein	30.2g
Fat	10.9g
Saturated fat	3.49g
Carbohydrate	9g
Fibre	1.3g
Sodium	142mg

Fruity Cider Pork with Parsley Dumplings

Pork, cider and fruit are a time-honoured combination. If you don't want to make dumplings, serve creamy mashed potatoes with the stew.

INGREDIENTS

Serves 6

115g/4oz/½ cup pitted prunes, roughly chopped
115g/4oz/½ cup dried apricots, roughly chopped
300ml/½ pint/1¼ cups dry cider
30ml/2 tbsp plain flour
675g/1½lb lean boneless pork, cut into cubes
30ml/2 tbsp oil
350g/12oz onions, roughly chopped
2 garlic cloves, crushed
6 celery sticks, roughly chopped
475ml/16fl oz/2 cups hot home-made chicken stock
12 juniper berries, lightly crushed
30ml/2 tbsp chopped fresh thyme
115g/4oz/1 cup self-raising flour
50g/2oz/generous ⅓ cup vegetable suet
45ml/3 tbsp chopped fresh parsley
425g/15oz can black-eyed beans, drained
freshly ground black pepper

1 Preheat the oven to 180°C/350°F/ Gas 4. Place the chopped prunes and apricots in a small bowl. Pour over the cider and leave to soak for at least 20 minutes.

2 Season 30ml/2 tbsp flour with pepper. Toss the pork in the plain flour to coat, and reserve any leftover flour. Heat the oil in a flameproof casserole. Brown the meat in batches, then remove from the casserole.

3 Add the onions, garlic and celery to the casserole and cook for about 5 minutes. Add any remaining flour and cook for 1 minute. Blend in the stock, cider and fruit, juniper berries, thyme and plenty of seasoning. Bring to the boil, add the pork, cover and cook in the oven for 50 minutes.

4 Just before the end of the cooking time prepare the dumplings. Sift the self-raising flour into a bowl, then stir in the suet and parsley. Add about 90ml/6 tbsp water and mix together to form a smooth dough.

5 Remove the casserole from the oven, stir in the beans and adjust the seasoning. Divide the dumpling mixture into six, form into rounds and place on top. Return to the oven, covered, and cook for a further 20–25 minutes, or until the dumplings are cooked and the pork is tender.

NUTRITION NOTES	
Per portion:	
Energy	487Kcals/2041kJ
Protein	33.3g
Fat	16.7g
Saturated fat	5.58g
Carbohydrate	51g
Fibre	6.3g
Sodium	254mg

Roast Leg of Lamb with Mushroom Stuffing

When the thigh bone is removed from a leg of lamb, a stuffing can be put in its place. This not only makes the joint easier to carve but also gives a wonderful flavour to the meat that lessens the need to add salt. Roast potatoes, carrots and broccoli are all excellent accompaniments.

INGREDIENTS

Serves 4

1.75kg/4-4½lb leg of lamb, boned
freshly ground black pepper
watercress, to garnish
lightly cooked carrots and broccoli
  and roast potatoes, to serve

For the stuffing

25g/1oz/2 tbsp unsalted butter
1 shallot or small onion, chopped
225g/8oz assorted wild and cultivated
  mushrooms, such as chanterelles,
  ceps, bay boletus, horn of plenty,
  blewits, oyster, St George's, field
  and Caesar's mushrooms, trimmed
  and chopped
½ garlic clove, crushed
1 fresh thyme sprig, chopped
25g/1oz saltless white bread, crust
  removed and diced
2 egg yolks

For the gravy

50ml/3½ tbsp red wine
400ml/14fl oz/1⅔ cups boiling home-
  made chicken stock
5g/⅙oz/2 tbsp dried ceps, bay boletus
  or saffron milk-caps, soaked in
  boiling water for 20 minutes
20ml/4 tsp cornflour
5ml/1 tsp mustard
2.5ml/½ tsp wine vinegar
a knob of unsalted butter

COOK'S TIP

If you buy your meat from a butcher, ask
for the thigh bone to be removed.

---

1 Preheat the oven to 200°C/400°F/ Gas 6. To make the stuffing, melt the butter in a large, non-stick frying pan and gently fry the shallot or onion without colouring.

2 Add the mushrooms, garlic and thyme, and stir the mixture until the mushroom juices begin to run, then increase the heat so that they evaporate completely.

3 Transfer the mushrooms to a large mixing bowl, add the bread, egg yolks and pepper, and mix well. Allow to cool slightly.

NUTRITION NOTES

Per portion:

Energy	967Kcals/4027kJ
Protein	87.1g
Fat	63.4g
Saturated fat	32.12g
Carbohydrate	10g
Fibre	0.9g
Sodium	322mg

4 Season the inside cavity of the lamb with pepper and then press the stuffing into the cavity, using a spoon or your fingers. Tie up the end with string and then tie around the joint to help it keep shape.

5 Place the lamb in a roasting tin and roast in the oven for 15 minutes per 450g/1lb for rare meat or 20 minutes per 450g/1lb for medium-rare. For this recipe, cook for 1 hour 20 minutes for medium-rare.

6 Transfer the lamb to a warmed serving plate, cover and keep warm. To make the gravy, spoon off all the excess fat from the roasting tin and brown the sediment over a moderate heat. Add the wine and stir with a flat wooden spoon to loosen the sediment. Add the chicken stock, the dried mushrooms and their soaking liquid.

7 Blend the cornflour and mustard with 15ml/1 tbsp water, stir into the stock and simmer to thicken. Add the vinegar. Season to taste and stir in the butter. Garnish the lamb with watercress and serve with vegetables.

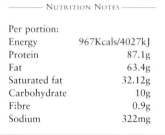

Irish Stew

The secret to the delicious flavour of this quintessential Irish main course is its simplicity. Traditionally, mutton chops are used, but as they are harder to find these days you can use lamb instead. A good accompaniment for Irish stew is Savoy cabbage.

INGREDIENTS

Serves 4

1.2kg/2½lb boneless lamb chops
15ml/1 tbsp vegetable oil
3 large onions, quartered
4 large carrots, thickly sliced
900ml/1½ pints/3¾ cups water
4 large potatoes
1 large sprig fresh thyme
15g/½oz/1 tbsp unsalted butter
15ml/1 tbsp chopped fresh parsley
freshly ground black pepper
Savoy cabbage, to serve (optional)

1 Using a sharp knife, trim any fat from the lamb and cut into cubes. Heat the oil in a flameproof casserole and brown the meat on both sides. Remove from the pan.

2 Add the onions and carrots to the casserole and cook for 5 minutes until the onions are browned. Return the meat to the pan with the water. Bring to the boil, reduce the heat, cover and simmer for 1 hour.

3 Cut the potatoes into chunks and add to the pan with the thyme. Cook very gently for 1 hour further.

4 Leave the stew to settle for a few minutes. Remove the fat from the liquid with a large spoon or ladle, then pour off the liquid into a large, clean saucepan.

5 Stir in the butter and the chopped parsley. Season well with pepper, mix well, and pour the liquid back into the casserole. Serve, accompanied by Savoy cabbage if you wish.

NUTRITION NOTES	
Per portion:	
Energy	693Kcals/2894kJ
Protein	48.8g
Fat	34.5g
Saturated fat	16.46g
Carbohydrate	50g
Fibre	6.8g
Sodium	160mg

Beef Tagine with Sweet Potatoes

This colourful, warming dish is just what is needed on cold winter nights. Only mildly spicy, leave in some of the chilli seeds for a little more zing.

INGREDIENTS

Serves 4

675–900g/1½–2lb stewing beef
30ml/2 tbsp sunflower oil
a good pinch of ground turmeric
1 large onion, chopped
1 red or green chilli, seeded
  and chopped
7.5ml/1½ tsp paprika
a good pinch of cayenne pepper
2.5ml/½ tsp ground cumin
450g/1lb sweet potatoes, sliced
15ml/1 tbsp chopped fresh parsley
15ml/1 tbsp chopped fresh coriander,
  plus extra to garnish
15g/½oz/1 tbsp unsalted butter
freshly ground black pepper

1 Trim the meat and cut into 2cm/¾ in cubes. Heat the oil in a flameproof casserole and fry the meat, together with the turmeric and pepper, over a medium heat for 3–4 minutes until evenly browned. With a wooden spoon, stir frequently to prevent the meat from sticking to the bottom of the pan.

2 Cover the pan tightly and cook for 15 minutes over a fairly gentle heat, without lifting the lid. Preheat the oven to 180°C/350°F/Gas 4.

3 Add the onion, chilli, paprika, cayenne pepper and cumin to the pan, together with just enough water to cover the meat. Cover tightly and cook in the oven for 1–1½ hours until the meat is very tender, checking occasionally and, if necessary, adding a little extra water to keep the stew fairly moist.

4 Transfer the sweet potatoes and water to a pan, bring to the boil and simmer for 2–3 minutes until just tender. Drain.

5 Add the herbs to the meat, plus a little extra water if the stew appears dry. Arrange the sweet potato slices over the meat and dot with butter. Cover and cook in the oven for a further 10 minutes, or until the potatoes feel very tender. Increase the oven temperature to 200°C/400°F/Gas 6 or heat the grill.

6 Remove the lid of the casserole and cook in the oven or under the grill for a further 5–10 minutes until golden. Garnish with coriander.

Pan-grilled Veal Chops

Veal chops from the loin are an expensive cut but are well worth it and are shown to their best advantage when cooked quickly and simply. The flavour of fresh basil goes well with veal, but other herbs can be used instead if you prefer.

INGREDIENTS

Serves 2
30ml/2 tbsp unsalted butter, softened
15ml/1 tbsp mustard
15ml/1 tbsp chopped fresh basil
olive oil, for brushing
2 veal loin chops, 2.5cm/1in thick (about 225g/8oz each)
freshly ground black pepper

1 Cream the butter with the mustard and chopped basil in a small bowl, then season to taste with pepper.

2 Lightly oil a heavy, cast iron skillet. Set over high heat until very hot but not smoking. Brush both sides of each chop with a little oil and season with a little pepper.

3 Place the chops on the skillet and reduce the heat to medium. Cook for about 5 minutes, then turn and cook for a further 3–4 minutes until done as preferred (medium-rare meat will still be slightly soft when pressed, medium meat will be springy and well-done firm). Top each chop with half the basil butter and serve at once.

———— NUTRITION NOTES ————

Per portion:
Energy	324Kcals/1359kJ
Protein	38.7g
Fat	18.3g
Saturated fat	8.6g
Carbohydrate	1g
Fibre	0g
Sodium	421mg

Veal Escalopes with Tarragon

Aromatic tarragon has long been popular for flavouring sauces.

INGREDIENTS

Serves 4
4 veal escalopes (115–150g/4–5oz each)
15ml/1 tbsp unsalted butter
30ml/2 tbsp brandy
250ml/8fl oz/1 cup home-made stock
15ml/1 tbsp chopped fresh tarragon
freshly ground black pepper
fresh tarragon sprigs, to garnish

———— NUTRITION NOTES ————

Per portion:
Energy	200Kcals/839kJ
Protein	25.3g
Fat	8.5g
Saturated fat	4.37g
Carbohydrate	1g
Fibre	0g
Sodium	135mg

1 Place the veal escalopes between two sheets of wax or greaseproof paper and pound with the flat side of a meat mallet or roll them with a rolling pin to flatten to about 5mm/¼in thickness. Season with pepper.

2 Melt the butter in a large frying pan over medium-high heat. Add enough meat to fit easily in one layer (cook in batches if necessary) and fry for 1½–2 minutes, turning once. Be careful not to overcook. Transfer to a plate and keep warm.

3 Add the brandy to the pan, then pour in the stock and bring to the boil. Add the chopped tarragon and continue to boil until the liquid is reduced by half. Return the veal to the pan with any accumulated juices and heat through. Serve immediately, garnished with tarragon sprigs.

———— COOK'S TIP ————

Take care not to overcook the veal as the thin slices cook very quickly.

Chicken with Tomatoes and Prawns

This Piedmontese dish was created especially for Napoleon. Versions of it appear in both Italian and French recipe books.

INGREDIENTS

Serves 4

120ml/4fl oz/½ cup olive oil
8 chicken thighs on the bone, skinned
1 onion, finely chopped
1 celery stick, finely chopped
1 garlic clove, crushed
350g/12oz ripe Italian plum tomatoes,
   peeled and roughly chopped
250ml/8fl oz/1 cup dry white wine
2.5ml/½ tsp chopped fresh rosemary
15ml/1 tbsp unsalted butter
8 small triangles thinly sliced saltless
   white bread, without crusts
175g/6oz large raw prawns, shelled
freshly ground black pepper
finely chopped flat-leaf parsley,
   to garnish

1 Heat about 30ml/2 tbsp of the oil in a frying pan. Add the chicken thighs and sauté over a medium heat for about 5 minutes until they have changed colour on all sides. Transfer to a flameproof casserole.

2 Add the onion and celery to the frying pan and cook gently, stirring frequently, for about 3 minutes until softened. Add the garlic, tomatoes, wine, rosemary and pepper to taste. Bring to the boil, stirring.

3 Pour the tomato sauce over the chicken. Cover and cook gently for 40 minutes, or until the chicken is tender when pierced.

4 About 10 minutes before serving, add the remaining oil and the butter to the frying pan and heat until hot but not smoking. Add the triangles of bread and shallow fry until crisp and golden on each side. Drain.

5 Add the prawns to the casserole and heat until the prawns are cooked. Taste the sauce for seasoning. Dip one of the tips of each fried bread triangle in parsley. Serve the dish hot, garnished with the bread triangles.

NUTRITION NOTES	
Per portion:	
Energy	659Kcals/2747kJ
Protein	57.2g
Fat	37.7g
Saturated fat	8.24g
Carbohydrate	14g
Fibre	1.7g
Sodium	380mg

Moroccan Harissa-spiced Roast Chicken

The spices and dried fruit in this stuffing give the roast chicken an unusual flavour and help to keep it moist.

INGREDIENTS

Serves 4–5

1.5kg/3–3½lb chicken
30–60ml/2–4 tbsp garlic and spice oil (*see* Cook's Tip)
a few bay leaves
10ml/2 tsp clear honey
10ml/2 tsp tomato purée
60ml/4 tbsp lemon juice
150ml/¼ pint/⅔ cup hot home-made chicken stock
2.5–5ml/½–1 tsp harissa

For the stuffing

25g/1oz/2 tbsp unsalted butter
1 onion, chopped
1 garlic clove, crushed
7.5ml/1½ tsp ground cinnamon
2.5ml/½ tsp ground cumin
225g/8oz/1⅓ cups dried fruit, soaked for several hours or overnight in water to cover
25g/1oz/¼ cup blanched almonds, finely chopped
freshly ground black pepper

1 Make the stuffing. Melt the butter in a saucepan. Add the chopped onion and garlic and cook gently for 5 minutes until soft. Add the ground cinnamon and cumin and cook, stirring, for 2 minutes.

2 Drain the dried fruit, chop it roughly and add to the stuffing with the almonds. Season with pepper and cook for 2 minutes more. Tip into a bowl and leave to cool.

3 Preheat the oven to 200°C/400°F/ Gas 6. Using a spoon, stuff the neck of the chicken with the fruit mixture, reserving any excess. Generously brush the garlic and spice oil all over the chicken. Place the chicken in a roasting tin, tuck in the bay leaves and roast for 1–1¼ hours, basting occasionally with the juices, until golden brown and well cooked.

4 Transfer the chicken to a carving board. Pour off any excess fat from the roasting tin. Stir the honey, tomato purée, lemon juice, stock and harissa into the juices in the tin. Bring to the boil and simmer for 2 minutes, stirring. Meanwhile, reheat any excess stuffing. Carve the chicken and serve with the stuffing and sauce.

COOK'S TIP

To make garlic and spice oil, steep garlic, bay leaves, mustard seeds, peppercorns and chillies in olive oil for 2 weeks.

NUTRITION NOTES

Per portion:

Energy	659Kcals/2747kJ
Protein	44.7g
Fat	34.1g
Saturated fat	10.81g
Carbohydrate	46g
Fibre	2.3g
Sodium	165mg

Aromatic Chicken

This is best cooked ahead so that the flavours permeate the chicken flesh, making it even more delicious. Serve cucumber alongside if you wish, which is the traditional accompaniment.

INGREDIENTS

Serves 4

1.5kg/3–3½lb chicken, quartered, or 4 chicken quarters
5ml/1 tsp sugar
30ml/2 tbsp coriander seeds
10ml/2 tsp cumin seeds
6 cloves
2.5ml/½ tsp ground nutmeg
2.5ml/½ tsp ground turmeric
1 small onion
2.5cm/1in fresh root ginger, peeled and sliced
300ml/½ pint/1¼ cups hot home-made chicken stock or water
freshly ground black pepper
boiled rice, to serve

1 Cut each chicken quarter in half to obtain eight pieces. Place in a flameproof casserole, sprinkle with sugar and toss together. This helps release the juices in the chicken. If using a whole chicken, use the back-bone and any remaining carcass to make the stock for this recipe, if liked.

2 Dry-fry the coriander, cumin and cloves until the spices give off a good aroma. Add the nutmeg and turmeric and heat briefly. Grind in a food processor or a pestle and mortar.

3 If using a processor, process the onion and ginger until finely chopped. Otherwise, finely chop the onion and ginger and pound to a paste with a pestle and mortar. Add the ground spices and chicken stock or water and mix well.

4 Pour the onion mixture over the chicken in the flameproof casserole. Cover with a lid and cook over a gentle heat for about 45–50 minutes until the chicken pieces are really tender.

5 Season with pepper to taste, then serve portions of the chicken, with the sauce, on boiled rice.

NUTRITION NOTES

Per portion:	
Energy	543Kcals/2258kJ
Protein	50.4g
Fat	35.9g
Saturated fat	10g
Carbohydrate	7g
Fibre	0.3g
Sodium	184mg

Prawn Curry

This is a rich, flavoursome curry made from succulent prawns and a delicious blend of aromatic spices.

INGREDIENTS

Serves 4

675g/1½lb raw tiger prawns
4 dried red chillies
50g/2oz/1 cup desiccated coconut
5ml/1 tsp black mustard seeds
1 large onion, chopped
45ml/3 tbsp oil
4 bay leaves
2.5cm/1in piece root ginger,
   finely chopped
2 garlic cloves, crushed
15ml/1 tbsp ground coriander
5ml/1 tsp chilli powder
4 tomatoes, finely chopped
boiled rice, to serve
unpeeled cooked prawns,
   to garnish

1 Peel the prawns. Run a sharp knife along the back of each prawn to make a shallow cut and carefully remove the thin, black intestinal vein.

— NUTRITION NOTES —	
Per portion:	
Energy	344Kcals/1429kJ
Protein	33.1g
Fat	18.7g
Saturated fat	7.78g
Carbohydrate	12g
Fibre	3.3g
Sodium	351mg

2 Put the dried red chillies, coconut, mustard seeds and onion in a large frying pan and dry-fry for about 8–10 minutes or until the mixture begins to brown. Put into a food processor or blender and process to a coarse paste.

3 Heat the oil in the frying pan and fry the bay leaves for 1 minute. Add the chopped ginger and the garlic and fry for 2–3 minutes.

4 Add the coriander and chilli and fry for about 5 minutes. Stir in the tomatoes and about 175ml/6fl oz/ ¾ cup water and simmer for 5–6 minutes, or until thickened.

5 Add the prawns and cook for about 4–5 minutes, or until they turn pink and the edges are curling slightly. Serve with boiled rice, garnished with unpeeled cooked prawns.

Trout with Almonds

This simple and quick recipe can also be made with hazelnuts.

INGREDIENTS

Serves 2

2 trout (350g/12oz each), cleaned
40g/1½oz/⅓ cup plain flour
50g/2oz/4 tbsp unsalted butter
25g/1oz/¼ cup sliced almonds
30ml/2 tbsp dry white wine
freshly ground black pepper

NUTRITION NOTES

Per portion:

Energy	636Kcals/2667kJ
Protein	46.3g
Fat	42.1g
Saturated fat	17.63g
Carbohydrate	17g
Fibre	1.7g
Sodium	100mg

1 Rinse the trout and pat dry. Put the flour in a large polythene bag and season with pepper. Place the trout, one at a time, in the bag and shake to coat with flour. Shake off the excess flour from the fish and discard the remaining flour.

2 Fry the trout in half the butter in a frying pan for 6–7 minutes on each side, until golden brown and cooked through. Transfer the fish to warmed plates and keep warm.

3 Add the remaining butter to the pan and cook the almonds until just lightly browned. Add the wine to the pan and boil for 1 minute, stirring constantly, until slightly syrupy. Pour or spoon over the fish and serve at once.

Tuna with Garlic, Tomatoes and Herbs

This Provençal dish owes its full flavour to the generous use of local herbs, such as thyme, rosemary and oregano, which grow wild on the hillsides and feature in many recipes from the region.

INGREDIENTS

Serves 4

4 tuna steaks, about 2.5cm/1in thick (175–200g/6–7oz each)
30–45ml/2–3 tbsp olive oil
3 or 4 garlic cloves, finely chopped
60ml/4 tbsp dry white wine
3 ripe plum tomatoes, peeled, seeded and chopped
5ml/1 tsp dried herbes de Provence
freshly ground black pepper
fresh basil leaves, to garnish
fried potatoes, to serve

1 Season the tuna steaks with pepper. Set a heavy frying pan over high heat until very hot, add the oil and swirl to coat.

2 Add the tuna steaks and press down gently, then reduce the heat to medium and cook for 6–8 minutes, turning once, until just slightly pink in the centre.

NUTRITION NOTES

Per portion:

Energy	313Kcals/1314kJ
Protein	42.4g
Fat	13.8g
Saturated fat	2.98g
Carbohydrate	3g
Fibre	1g
Sodium	90mg

3 Transfer the steaks to a serving plate, cover and keep warm. Add the garlic to the pan and fry for 15–20 seconds, stirring all the time, then pour in the wine and boil until it is reduced by half. Add the tomatoes and dried herbs and cook for 2–3 minutes until the sauce is bubbling. Season with pepper and pour over the fish steaks. Serve garnished with fresh basil leaves and accompanied by fried potatoes.

Provençal Vegetable Stew

This classic combination of the vegetables that grow abundantly in the South of France is infinitely flexible. Use the recipe as a guide for making the most of what you have on hand.

INGREDIENTS

Serves 6

2 medium aubergines (about 450g/1b total weight)
60–75ml/4–5 tbsp olive oil
1 large onion, halved and sliced
2 or 3 garlic cloves, very finely chopped
1 large red or yellow pepper, peeled, seeded and cut into thin strips
2 large courgettes, cut into 1cm/½in slices
675g/1½lb ripe tomatoes, peeled, seeded and chopped, or 400g/14oz can chopped tomatoes
5ml/1 tsp dried herbes de Provence, such as rosemary, thyme and oregano
freshly ground black pepper

1 Preheat the grill. Cut the aubergine into 2cm/¾in slices, then brush the slices with olive oil on both sides and grill until lightly browned, turning once. Cut the slices into cubes.

2 Heat 15ml/1 tbsp of the olive oil in a flameproof casserole and cook the onion over a medium-low heat for about 10 minutes until lightly golden, stirring frequently. Add the garlic, the peppers and courgettes and cook for 10 minutes, stirring occasionally.

3 Add the tomatoes and aubergine cubes, dried herbs and ground pepper, and simmer gently, covered, over a low heat for about 20 minutes, stirring from time to time. Uncover and continue cooking for a further 20–25 minutes, stirring occasionally, until all the vegetables are tender and the cooking liquid has thickened. Serve hot or at room temperature.

COOK'S TIP

To peel the pepper, quarter and grill, skin side up, until blackened. Enclose in a polythene bag and set aside until cool. Peel off the skin, then remove the core and seeds.

NUTRITION NOTES

Per portion:

Energy	139Kcals/576kJ
Protein	3.9g
Fat	8.5g
Saturated fat	1.13g
Carbohydrate	13g
Fibre	4.6g
Sodium	41mg

Spiced Tofu Stir-fry

You could add any quickly cooked vegetable to this stir-fry – try mangetouts, sugar snap peas, leeks or thin slices of carrot. The lime juice and honey add flavour in place of high-salt sauces.

INGREDIENTS

Serves 4

10ml/2 tsp ground cumin
15ml/1 tbsp paprika
5ml/1 tsp ground ginger
a good pinch of cayenne pepper
15ml/1 tbsp caster sugar
275g/10oz firm tofu (beancurd)
60ml/4 tbsp oil
2 garlic cloves, crushed
1 bunch spring onions, sliced
1 red pepper, seeded and sliced
1 yellow pepper, seeded and sliced
225g/8oz/generous 3 cups brown-cap
   mushrooms, halved or quartered
   if necessary
1 large courgette, sliced
115g/4oz fine green beans, halved
50g/2oz/scant ½ cup pine nuts
15ml/1 tbsp lime juice
15ml/1 tbsp clear honey
freshly ground black pepper

1 Mix together the cumin, paprika, ginger, cayenne and sugar with plenty of black pepper. Cut the tofu into cubes and toss them gently in the spice mixture to coat.

2 Heat half the oil in a wok or large frying pan. Cook the tofu over a high heat for 3–4 minutes, turning occasionally (take care not to break up the tofu too much).

3 Remove with a slotted spoon and set aside. Wipe out the pan with kitchen paper.

4 Add the remaining oil to the pan and cook the garlic and spring onions for 3 minutes. Add the remaining vegetables and cook over a medium heat for 6 minutes, or until beginning to soften and turn golden. Season well.

5 Return the tofu to the pan with the pine nuts, lime juice and honey. Heat through thoroughly and serve immediately.

NUTRITION NOTES	
Per portion:	
Energy	339Kcals/1406kJ
Protein	11.8g
Fat	24.4g
Saturated fat	2.79g
Carbohydrate	19g
Fibre	3.5g
Sodium	17mg

PASTA, PIZZA AND GRAINS

The backbone of so many meals, the carbohydrate element of your cooking

is of great importance to your health. Your tastebuds will approve, too, as

you discover new and interesting combinations and toppings. Try pasta dishes

such as Tagliatelle with Milanese Sauce, rice dishes such as Shellfish Risotto

with Fruits of the Forest, or recipes using more unusual grains such as

Lamb and Pumpkin Couscous and Bulgur Wheat and Lentil Pilaff.

Pasta Shells with Tomato and Tuna Sauce

Don't be tempted to shorten the cooking time for the sauce: the long cooking time makes for a richer flavour.

INGREDIENTS

Serves 6
1 medium onion, finely chopped
1 celery stick, finely chopped
1 red pepper, seeded and diced
1 garlic clove, crushed
150ml/¼ pint/⅔ cup hot home-made
    chicken stock
400g/14oz can chopped tomatoes
15ml/1 tbsp tomato purée
10ml/2 tsp caster sugar
15ml/1 tbsp chopped fresh basil
15ml/1 tbsp chopped fresh parsley
450g/1lb dried pasta shells
400g/14oz can tuna in oil, drained
30ml/2 tbsp capers in vinegar, drained
freshly ground black pepper

1 Put the chopped onion, celery, red pepper and garlic into a non-stick pan. Add the stock, bring to the boil and cook for 5 minutes, or until the stock has reduced almost completely.

2 Add the tomatoes, tomato purée, sugar and herbs. Season to taste with ground pepper and bring to the boil. Simmer for 30 minutes until thick, stirring occasionally.

3 Meanwhile, cook the pasta in a large pan of boiling water according to the packet instructions. Drain thoroughly and transfer to a warm serving dish.

4 Flake the tuna into large chunks and add to the sauce with the capers. Heat gently for 1-2 minutes, pour over the pasta, toss gently and serve immediately.

NUTRITION NOTES	
Per portion:	
Energy	353Kcals/1504kJ
Protein	23.4g
Fat	1.9g
Saturated fat	0.32g
Carbohydrate	65g
Fibre	3.8g
Sodium	279mg

Tagliatelle with Milanese Sauce

Serve this with a green salad for a substantial, healthy supper.

INGREDIENTS

Serves 4

1 onion, finely chopped
1 celery stick, finely chopped
1 red pepper, seeded and diced
1–2 garlic cloves, crushed
150ml/¼ pint/⅔ cup home-made
  vegetable stock
400g/14oz can tomatoes
15ml/1 tbsp concentrated
  tomato purée
10ml/2 tsp caster sugar
5ml/1 tsp dried mixed herbs
350g/12oz tagliatelle
115g/4oz/1½ cups button
  mushrooms, sliced
60ml/4 tbsp white wine
115g/4oz lean cooked ham, diced
freshly ground black pepper
chopped fresh parsley, to garnish

1 Put the onion, celery, red pepper and garlic into a non-stick pan. Add the stock, bring to the boil and cook for 5 minutes, or until tender.

2 Add the tomatoes, tomato purée, sugar and dried herbs. Season with ground pepper. Bring to the boil and simmer for 30 minutes until thick. Stir occasionally.

3 Cook the pasta in a large pan of boiling water until *al dente*. Drain thoroughly and set aside.

4 Put the mushrooms in to a pan with the white wine, cover and cook for 3–4 minutes until tender and all the wine has been absorbed.

5 Add the mushrooms and diced ham to the tomato sauce. Reheat.

6 Transfer the pasta to a warmed serving dish and spoon on the sauce. Garnish with chopped parsley.

NUTRITION NOTES	
Per portion:	
Energy	297Kcals/1243kJ
Protein	17.1g
Fat	3.2g
Saturated fat	0.69g
Carbohydrate	51g
Fibre	5g
Sodium	414mg

Baked Seafood Spaghetti

In this dish, each seafood portion is baked and then served in an individual packet to be opened at the table. For best results, make the packets using aluminium foil or baking parchment.

INGREDIENTS

Serves 4
450g/1lb fresh mussels
120ml/4fl oz/½ cup dry white wine
60ml/4 tbsp olive oil
2 garlic cloves, finely chopped
450g/1lb tomatoes, fresh or canned, peeled and finely chopped
400g/14oz spaghetti or other long pasta
90g/3½oz peeled and deveined raw prawns, fresh or frozen
30ml/2 tbsp chopped fresh parsley
freshly ground black pepper

1 Scrub the mussels well under cold running water, cutting off the "beard" with a small, sharp knife. Place the mussels and dry white wine in a large saucepan and gently heat until they open.

NUTRITION NOTES

Per portion:
Energy	530Kcals/2238kJ
Protein	22.9g
Fat	14g
Saturated fat	2g
Carbohydrate	79g
Fibre	4.4g
Sodium	511mg

2 Lift out the mussels and set aside. (Discard any that have not opened.) Strain the cooking liquid through kitchen paper, and reserve. Preheat the oven to 150°C/300°F/Gas 2.

3 In a saucepan, heat the oil and garlic together for 1–2 minutes. Add the tomatoes and cook until they soften. Stir in 175ml/6fl oz/¾ cup of the cooking liquid from the mussels. Cook the pasta in boiling water until *al dente.*

4 Just before draining the pasta, add the prawns and parsley to the tomato sauce. Cook for 2 minutes. Taste for seasoning, adding pepper as desired. Remove from the heat.

5 Drain the pasta and place in a bowl. Add the tomato sauce and mix well. Stir in the mussels. Prepare four pieces of baking parchment or foil approximately 30 x 45cm (12 x 18in). Place each sheet in the centre of a shallow bowl.

6 Divide the pasta and seafood among the four pieces of paper, placing a mound in the centre of each, and twist the paper ends together to make a closed packet. (The bowl under the paper will stop the sauce from spilling while the paper parcels are being closed.)

7 Arrange on a large baking sheet and place in the centre of the oven. Bake for 8–10 minutes. Place one unopened packet on each individual serving plate.

VARIATION

Prawns naturally contain salt, so reserve this dish for special occasions only. You can also substitute the prawns for cod for a dish that will be virtually salt-free.

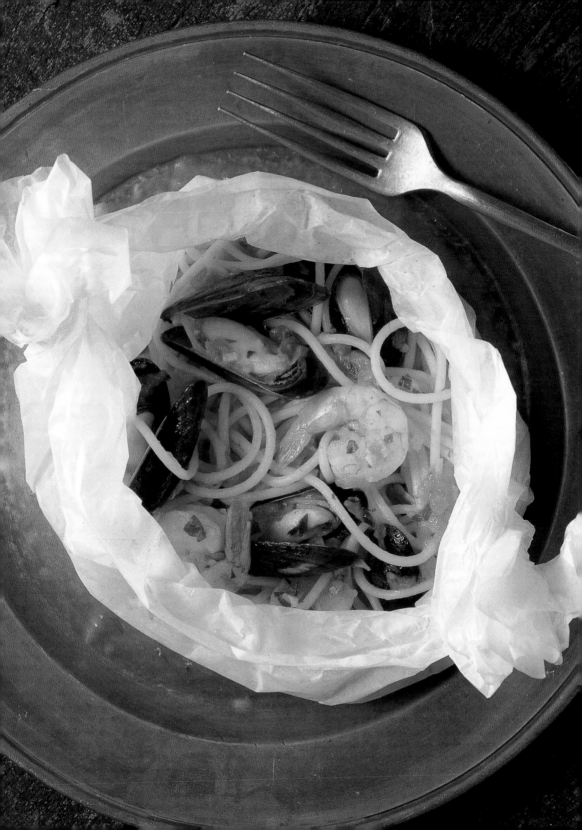

Vegetarian Fried Noodles

Colour, texture and flavour all play a part in this quick and easy vegetarian dish.

Ingredients

Serves 4

2 eggs
5ml/1 tsp chilli powder
5ml/1 tsp ground turmeric
60ml/4 tbsp vegetable oil
1 large onion, finely sliced
2 red chillies, seeded and
    finely sliced
2 medium potatoes, cubed
6 pieces fried tofu (beancurd), sliced,
    about 225g/8oz
225g/8oz/1 cup beansprouts
115g/4oz green beans, blanched
350g/12oz fresh thick egg noodles
freshly ground black pepper
sliced spring onions, to garnish

1 Beat the eggs lightly, then strain them into a bowl. Heat a lightly greased omelette pan. Pour in half of the egg to cover the bottom of the pan thinly.

2 When the egg is just set, turn the omelette over and fry briefly on the other side. Slide on to a plate, blot with kitchen paper, roll up and cut into narrow strips. Make a second omelette in the same way and slice. Set aside the omelette strips to use for garnishing the finished dish.

3 In a cup, mix together the chilli powder and turmeric. Form a paste by stirring in a little water.

4 Heat the oil in a wok or large frying pan. Fry the onion until soft. Reduce the heat and add the chilli paste and sliced chillies. Fry for 2–3 minutes, stirring occasionally.

5 Add the potato cubes and fry for about 2 minutes, mixing well with the chillies. Add the beancurd, then the beansprouts, green beans and egg noodles, stirring frequently.

6 Gently stir-fry until the noodles are evenly coated and heated through. Take care not to break up the potatoes or the beancurd. Season with pepper to taste. Serve hot, garnished with the reserved omelette strips and spring onion slices.

Cook's Tip

Always be very careful when handling chillies. Keep your hands away from your eyes as the juice from chillies will sting them, and wash your hands thoroughly after touching chillies.

Nutrition Notes

Per portion:

Energy	613Kcals/2571kJ
Protein	24.2g
Fat	27.1g
Saturated fat	3.14g
Carbohydrate	73g
Fibre	2.6g
Sodium	218mg

Pizza with Fresh Vegetables

This pizza can be made with any combination of fresh vegetables.

INGREDIENTS

Serves 4

400g/14oz peeled plum tomatoes, fresh or canned, weighed whole, without extra juice
2 medium broccoli spears
225g/8oz asparagus
3 small courgettes
75ml/5 tbsp olive oil
50g/2oz/⅓ cup shelled peas, fresh or frozen
4 spring onions. sliced
1 quantity basic pizza dough, rolled out into 4 x 13cm/5in roundels
75g/3oz/¾ cup mozzarella cheese, cut into small dice
10 fresh basil leaves, torn into pieces
2 garlic cloves, finely chopped
freshly ground black pepper

1 Preheat the oven to 240°C/475°F/ Gas 9 for at least 20 minutes before baking the pizza. Strain the tomatoes through the medium holes of a food mill placed over a bowl, scraping in all the pulp.

2 With a sharp knife, peel the broccoli stems and asparagus and blanch with the courgettes in a large pan of boiling water for 4–5 minutes. Drain. Cut into bite-size pieces.

3 Heat 30ml/2 tbsp of the olive oil in a small pan. Stir in the peas and spring onions and cook for about 5–6 minutes, stirring frequently. Remove from the heat.

4 Spread the puréed tomatoes all over the pizza dough, leaving just the rim uncovered. Add the other vegetables, arranging them evenly on top of the tomatoes.

5 Sprinkle with the mozzarella, basil, garlic and pepper, and the remaining olive oil. Immediately place the pizza in the oven. Bake for about 20 minutes, or until the crust is golden brown and the cheese has melted.

NUTRITION NOTES	
Per portion:	
Energy	424Kcals/1770kJ
Protein	17.2g
Fat	22.6g
Saturated fat	5.05g
Carbohydrate	40g
Fibre	6.3g
Sodium	134mg

Prawn, Sun-dried Tomato and Basil Pizzettes

Slices of sun-dried tomatoes, with their concentrated, caramelized tomato flavour, make an excellent, easy topping for pizzas. Serve these pretty pizzettes as an appetizer or tasty snack.

INGREDIENTS

Serves 4

1 quantity basic pizza dough, rolled out
30ml/2 tbsp chilli oil
75g/3oz/¾ cup mozzarella cheese, grated
1 garlic clove, chopped
½ small red onion, thinly sliced
4–6 pieces sun-dried tomatoes, thinly sliced
115g/4oz cooked peeled prawns
30ml/2 tbsp chopped fresh basil
freshly ground black pepper
shredded basil leaves, to garnish

1 Preheat the oven to 220°/425°F/ Gas 7. Divide the rolled out dough into eight pieces.

2 Roll out each one on a lightly floured surface to a small oval about 5mm/¼in thick. Place well apart on two greased baking sheets. Prick all over with a fork.

3 Brush the bases with 15ml/1 tbsp of the chilli oil and top with the mozzarella, leaving a 1cm/½in border.

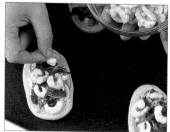

4 Divide the chopped garlic, onion, sun-dried tomatoes, prawns and chopped basil among the pizza bases. Season with pepper and drizzle the remaining chilli oil over the top. Bake for about 10 minutes until crisp and golden. Garnish with the shredded basil leaves and serve immediately.

Shellfish Risotto with Fruits of the Forest

A perfect combination of creamy Italian rice, mixed mushrooms and seafood.

INGREDIENTS

Serves 4

45ml/3 tbsp olive oil
1 medium onion, chopped
225g/8oz assorted wild and cultivated
   mushrooms such as ceps, bay boletus,
   and truffles, trimmed and sliced
450g/1lb/2¼ cups short-grain arborio
   or carnaroli rice
1.2 litres/2 pints/5 cups boiling home-
   made chicken or vegetable stock
150ml/¼ pint/⅔ cup white wine
115g/4oz raw prawns, peeled
225g/8oz mussels
225g/8oz Venus or carpet shell clams
1 medium squid, cleaned, trimmed
   and sliced
3 drops truffle oil (optional)
75ml/5 tbsp chopped fresh parsley
   and chervil
cayenne pepper, to taste

1 Heat the oil in a large frying pan and fry the onion for 6–8 minutes until soft but not brown.

2 Add the mushrooms and soften until their juices begin to run. Stir in the rice and heat through.

COOK'S TIP

Before cooking, tap the shellfish with a knife. Discard any shells that do not close. After cooking, discard any unopened shells.

3 Pour in the stock and white wine. Add the raw prawns, mussels, clams and squid, stir and gently simmer for about 15 minutes.

4 Add the truffle oil, if using, stir in the herbs, cover and stand for 5–10 minutes. Season to taste with cayenne pepper and serve.

NUTRITION NOTES

Per portion:

Energy	594Kcals/2481kJ
Protein	32.6g
Fat	12g
Saturated fat	1.35g
Carbohydrate	89g
Fibre	1.7g
Sodium	293mg

Thai Fried Rice

This recipe uses jasmine rice, which is sometimes known as Thai fragrant rice, adding to the dish a lovely subtle flavour.

INGREDIENTS

Serves 4

50g/2oz/½ cup coconut
 milk powder
375g/12oz/1⅔ cups jasmine rice
30ml/2 tbsp groundnut oil
2 garlic cloves, chopped
1 small onion, finely chopped
2.5cm/1in piece fresh root
 ginger, grated
225g/8oz boneless, skinless chicken
 breasts, cut into 1cm/½in dice
1 red pepper, seeded and diced
115g/4oz drained canned
 sweetcorn kernels
5ml/1 tsp chilli oil
15ml/1 tbsp hot curry powder
2 eggs, beaten
spring onion shreds, to garnish

1 In a saucepan, whisk the coconut milk powder into 475ml/16fl oz/2 cups water. Add the rice, bring to the boil and stir once. Lower the heat to a gentle simmer, cover and cook for 10 minutes, or until the rice is tender and the liquid has been absorbed. Spread the rice on a baking sheet and leave until completely cold.

2 Heat the oil in a wok, add the garlic, onion and ginger and stir-fry for 2 minutes.

3 Push the vegetables to the sides of the wok, add the chicken to the centre and stir-fry for 2 minutes. Add the rice and stir-fry over a high heat for 3 minutes more.

COOK'S TIP

It is important that you allow enough time for the rice to cool completely before it is fried. The oil also needs to be very hot, or the rice will absorb too much oil.

NUTRITION NOTES

Per portion:

Energy	554Kcals/2317kJ
Protein	25.9g
Fat	11.3g
Saturated fat	2.15g
Carbohydrate	93g
Fibre	2.3g
Sodium	296mg

4 Stir in the red pepper, sweetcorn, chilli oil and curry powder. Toss over the heat for 1 minute. Stir in the beaten eggs and cook for 1 minute more. Garnish with spring onion shreds and serve.

Lamb and Pumpkin Couscous

A traditional Moroccan-style dish marrying succulent meat, sweet vegetables and dried fruit with aromatic spices to produce a really satisfying dish.

INGREDIENTS

Serves 4–6

75g/3oz/½ cup chick-peas, soaked overnight
675g/1½lb lean lamb, cut into bite-size pieces
2 Spanish onions, sliced
a pinch of saffron
1.5ml/¼ tsp ground ginger
2.5ml/½ tsp ground turmeric
5ml/1 tsp ground black pepper
450g/1lb carrots
675g/1½lb pumpkin
75g/3oz/⅔ cup raisins
400g/14oz/2 cups couscous
fresh parsley, to garnish

1 Drain the chick-peas and cook in boiling water for 1–1½ hours until tender. Place in cold water and remove the skins by rubbing with your fingers. Discard the skins and drain.

2 Place the lamb, onions, saffron, ginger, turmeric, pepper and 1.2 litres/2 pints/5 cups water in a large saucepan. Slowly bring to the boil, then cover and simmer for about 1 hour until tender.

3 Meanwhile, prepare the vegetables. Peel the carrots and roughly cut into 6cm/2½ in pieces. Cut the pumpkin into 2.5cm/1in cubes, discarding the skin, seeds and pith.

4 Stir the carrots, pumpkin and raisins into the meat mixture, cover the pan and simmer for a further 30–35 minutes until the vegetables and meat are completely tender.

5 Prepare the couscous according to the instructions on the packet. Spoon on to a large warmed serving plate and ladle the stew on top. Garnish with parsley and serve.

NUTRITION NOTES	
Per portion:	
Energy	695Kcals/2911kJ
Protein	47g
Fat	16.9g
Saturated fat	7.77g
Carbohydrate	93g
Fibre	7.4g
Sodium	197mg

Bulgur Wheat and Lentil Pilaff

Bulgur wheat is a useful store-cupboard ingredient. It has a nutty taste and texture and only needs soaking before serving in a salad or warming through for a hot dish.

INGREDIENTS

Serves 4

115g/4oz/½ cup green lentils
115g/4oz/⅔ cup bulgur wheat
5ml/1 tsp ground coriander
5ml/1 tsp ground cinnamon
475ml/16fl oz/2 cups water
15ml/1 tbsp olive oil
225g/8oz rindless low-salt streaky
    bacon rashers, chopped
1 red onion, chopped
1 garlic clove, crushed
5ml/1 tsp cumin seeds
30ml/2 tbsp roughly chopped
    fresh parsley
freshly ground black pepper

1 Soak the lentils and bulgur wheat in separate clean, large bowls with plenty of cold water for about 1 hour. Drain thoroughly.

— NUTRITION NOTES —	
Per portion:	
Energy	357Kcals/1496kJ
Protein	20.4g
Fat	12.1g
Saturated fat	3.5g
Carbohydrate	44g
Fibre	3g
Sodium	437mg

2 Tip the lentils into a pan. Stir in the coriander, cinnamon and the water. Bring to the boil and simmer until the lentils are tender and the liquid has been absorbed.

3 Meanwhile, heat the olive oil and fry the bacon until crisp. Remove and drain on kitchen paper. Add the onion and garlic to the oil remaining in the pan and fry for 10 minutes until soft and golden brown. Stir in the cumin and cook for 1 minute more. Return the bacon to the pan.

4 Stir the drained bulgur wheat into the cooked lentils, then add the mixture to the frying pan. Season with pepper and heat through. Stir in the parsley and serve.

— COOK'S TIP —
If possible, use Puy lentils, which have a superior flavour, aroma and texture.

BREADS AND BAKING

You may not normally regard yourself as much of a baker, but try these inter-esting breads and have a go at these wonderful cakes, and you'll soon change your mind. Traditionally, breads and baking have required generous amounts of salt, and this is still true of those most ready-made ones. It is possible, however, to greatly reduce the amount of salt needed and still achieve delicious results. Try Tuscan No-salt Bread, for example, or treat yourself to some sumptuous Sticky Chocolate, Maple and Walnut Swirls.

Tuscan No-salt Bread

This bread from Tuscany is made without salt and probably originates from the days when salt was heavily taxed.

INGREDIENTS

Makes 1 loaf
500g/1¼lb/5 cups strong unbleached white bread flour
350ml/12fl oz/1½ cups boiling water
15g/½oz fresh yeast
60ml/4 tbsp lukewarm water

NUTRITION NOTES	
Per loaf:	
Energy	1883Kcals/8014kJ
Protein	65g
Fat	7.8g
Saturated fat	1.08g
Carbohydrate	414g
Fibre	17g
Sodium	34mg

1 First make the starter. Sift 175g/6oz/1½ cups of the flour into a large bowl. Pour over the boiling water, leave for a couple of minutes, then mix well. Cover with a damp dish towel and leave for 10 hours.

2 Lightly flour a baking sheet. Cream the yeast with the lukewarm water. Stir into the starter.

3 Gradually add the remaining flour and mix to form a dough. Turn out on to a lightly floured surface and knead for 5–8 minutes until elastic.

4 Place in a lightly oiled bowl, cover with lightly oiled clear film and leave to rise, in a warm place, for 1–1½ hours, or until doubled in bulk.

5 Turn out the dough on to a lightly floured surface, knock back and shape into a round.

6 Fold the sides of the round into the centre and seal. Place seam side up on the prepared baking sheet. Cover with lightly oiled clear film and leave to rise, in a warm place, for 30–45 minutes, or until doubled in size.

7 Flatten the loaf to about half its risen size and flip over. Cover with a large upturned bowl and leave to rise, in a warm place, for 30 minutes.

8 Meanwhile, preheat the oven to 220°C/425°F/Gas 7. Slash the top of the loaf, using a sharp knife, if wished. Bake for 30–35 minutes or until a light golden colour. Transfer to a wire rack to cool.

Spiced Naan Bread

The many seeds and the yogurt used in this recipe provide ample flavour, allowing you to avoid using salt. Traditionally baked in a fiercely hot tandoori oven, good results can also be achieved by using a hot oven and a grill.

INGREDIENTS

Makes 6

450g/1lb/4 cups plain flour
5ml/1 tsp baking powder
1 sachet easy-blend dried yeast
5ml/1 tsp caster sugar
5ml/1 tsp fennel seeds
10ml/2 tsp black onion seeds
5ml/1 tsp cumin seeds
150ml/¼ pint/⅔ cup hand-hot milk
30ml/2 tbsp oil, plus extra
    for brushing
150ml/¼ pint/⅔ cup plain yogurt
1 egg, beaten

1 Sift the flour and baking powder into a mixing bowl. Stir in the yeast, sugar, fennel seeds, black onion seeds and cumin seeds. Make a well in the centre. Stir the hand-hot milk into the flour mixture, then add the oil, yogurt and beaten egg. Mix to form a ball of dough.

2 Turn out the dough on to a lightly floured surface and knead it for 10 minutes until smooth. Return to the clean, lightly oiled bowl and roll the dough to coat it with oil. Cover the bowl with clear film and set aside until the dough has doubled in bulk.

3 Put a heavy baking sheet in the oven and preheat the oven to 240°C/475°F/Gas 9. Knead the dough again lightly and divide it into six pieces. Keep five pieces covered while working with the sixth.

4 Quickly roll the piece of dough out to a tear-drop shape, brush lightly with oil and slap the naan on to the hot baking sheet. Repeat with the remaining dough.

5 Preheat the grill. Bake the naan in the oven for 3 minutes until puffed up, then place the baking sheet under the grill for about 30 seconds, or until the naan are lightly browned. Serve hot or warm as an accompaniment to an Indian curry.

NUTRITION NOTES	
Per portion:	
Energy	355Kcals/1500kJ
Protein	11.2g
Fat	8g
Saturated fat	1.67g
Carbohydrate	64g
Fibre	2.3g
Sodium	150mg

VARIATION
Vary the spices used by adding chopped chilli to the mixture, or sprinkling the naan with poppy seeds before baking.

Sun-dried Tomato Bread

A delicious bread from the south of Italy. The combination of tomatoes and milk produce a lovely sweet bread that does not require the addition of salt.

INGREDIENTS

Makes 4 small loaves
675g/1½lb/6 cups strong white
   bread flour
25g/1oz/2 tbsp caster sugar
25g/1oz fresh yeast
400–475ml/14–16fl oz/1¾–2 cups
   warm milk
15ml/1 tbsp tomato purée
75ml/5 tbsp oil from the jar of
   sun-dried tomatoes
75ml/5 tbsp extra virgin olive oil
75g/3oz/¾ cup drained sun-dried
   tomatoes in oil, chopped
1 large onion, chopped

1 Sift the flour and sugar into a bowl and make a well in the centre. Crumble the yeast, mix with 150ml/ ¼ pint/⅔ cup of the warm milk and add to the flour.

2 Mix the tomato purée into the remaining milk until evenly blended, then add to the flour with the tomato oil and olive oil.

3 Gradually mix the flour into the liquid ingredients until you have a dough. Turn out on to a floured surface and knead for about 10 minutes until smooth and elastic. Return to the clean bowl, cover with a cloth and leave to rise in a warm place for about 2 hours.

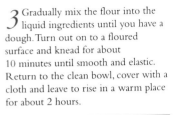

4 Knock the dough back and add the tomatoes and onion. Knead until evenly distributed through the dough. Shape into four rounds and place on a greased baking sheet. Cover with a dish towel and leave to rise again for about 45 minutes.

5 Preheat the oven to 190°C/375°F/ Gas 5. Bake the bread for 45 minutes, or until the loaves sound hollow when you tap them underneath with your fingers. Leave to cool for a few minutes on a wire rack before eating warm.

— NUTRITION NOTES —	
Per loaf:	
Energy	971Kcals/4087kJ
Protein	24.9g
Fat	36.5g
Saturated fat	6.85g
Carbohydrate	145g
Fibre	7.3g
Sodium	353mg

Irish Whiskey Cake

This moist, rich-tasting fruit cake is drizzled with whiskey as soon as it comes out of the oven.

INGREDIENTS

Serves 12

115g/4oz/½ cup glacé cherries
175g/6oz/¾ cup dark muscovado sugar
115g/4oz/⅔ cup sultanas
115g/4oz/⅔ cup raisins
115g/4oz/½ cup currants
300ml/½ pint/1¼ cups cold tea
300g/11oz/2½ cups plain self-raising
   flour, sifted
2 eggs
45ml/3 tbsp Irish whiskey

1 Mix the glacé cherries, muscovado sugar, dried fruit and tea in a large bowl. Leave to soak overnight until all the tea has been completely absorbed into the fruit.

2 Preheat the oven to 180°C/350°F/Gas 4. Grease and line a 1kg/2¼lb loaf tin. Add the flour, then the eggs to the fruit mixture and beat thoroughly until well mixed.

3 Pour the mixture into the prepared tin and bake for 1½ hours.

NUTRITION NOTES	
Per portion:	
Energy	257Kcals/1085kJ
Protein	3.6g
Fat	0.9g
Saturated fat	0.24g
Carbohydrate	60g
Fibre	1.4g
Sodium	108mg

4 Evenly prick the top of the cake with a skewer and drizzle over the whiskey while the cake is still hot. Allow to stand for about 5 minutes, then remove from the tin and cool on a wire rack.

COOK'S TIP

If time is short, use hot tea and soak the fruit for just 2 hours.

Pear and Sultana Teabread

This is an ideal teabread to make when pears are plentiful – an excellent use for windfalls.

INGREDIENTS

Serves 6–8
25g/1oz/scant ⅓ cup rolled oats
50g/2oz/¼ cup light
   muscovado sugar
30ml/2 tbsp pear or apple juice
30ml/2 tbsp sunflower oil
1 large or 2 small pears
115g/4oz/1 cup self-raising flour
115g/4oz/⅔ cup sultanas
2.5ml/½ tsp baking powder
10ml/2 tsp ground mixed spice
1 egg

1 Preheat the oven to 180°C/350°F/ Gas 4. Grease a 450g/1lb loaf tin and line with non-stick baking paper. Put the oats in a large, clean bowl with the sugar, pour over the pear or apple juice and oil, mix well and leave to stand for 15 minutes.

2 Quarter, core and grate the pear(s). Add to the oat mixture with the flour, sultanas, baking powder, mixed spice and egg, then mix together thoroughly.

3 Using a wooden spoon, transfer the mixture into the prepared loaf tin and level the top. Bake for 50–60 minutes or until a skewer inserted into the centre comes out clean.

4 Transfer the teabread to a wire rack and peel off the lining paper. Leave to cool completely.

NUTRITION NOTES

Per portion:

Energy	230Kcals/971kJ
Protein	4g
Fat	5.4g
Saturated fat	0.93g
Carbohydrate	44g
Fibre	1.9g
Sodium	138mg

Date and Apple Muffins

You will only need one or two of these wholesome muffins per person as they are very filling.

INGREDIENTS

Makes 12

150g/5oz/1¼ cups self-raising
   wholemeal flour
150g/5oz/1¼ cups self-raising
   white flour
5ml/1 tsp ground cinnamon
5ml/1 tsp baking powder
25g/1oz/2 tbsp soft margarine
75g/3oz/⅓ cup light muscovado sugar
1 eating apple
250ml/8fl oz/1 cup apple juice
30ml/2 tbsp pear and apple spread
1 egg, beaten
75g/3oz/½ cup chopped dates
15ml/1 tbsp chopped pecan nuts

1 Preheat the oven to 200°C/400°F/ Gas 6. Arrange 12 paper cases in a deep muffin tin. Sift the flours, cinnamon and baking powder into a bowl. Rub in the margarine until the mixture resembles breadcrumbs, then stir in the muscovado sugar.

NUTRITION NOTES

Per portion:

Energy	167Kcals/706kJ
Protein	3.7g
Fat	3.5g
Saturated fat	0.55g
Carbohydrate	32g
Fibre	2g
Sodium	119mg

2 Quarter and core the apple, chop the flesh finely and set aside. Stir a little of the apple juice with the pear and apple spread until smooth. Mix in the remaining juice, then add to the rubbed-in mixture with the egg. Add the chopped apple to the bowl with the dates. Fold in quickly until just combined – do not overmix.

3 Evenly divide the mixtures among the muffin cases.

4 Sprinkle with the chopped pecan nuts. Bake the muffins for 20–25 minutes until golden brown and firm in the middle. Remove to a wire rack and serve while still warm.

Stollen

Dating from the 12th century, and symbolizing the Holy Child wrapped in cloth, this traditional German Christmas cake is made from a rich yeast dough with marzipan and plenty of mixed dried fruits.

INGREDIENTS

Serves 12

350g/12oz/3 cups strong white
   bread flour
50g/2oz/⅓ cup caster sugar
10ml/2 tsp easy-blend dried yeast
150ml/¼ pint/⅔ cup milk
115g/4oz/½ cup butter
1 egg, beaten
175g/6oz/1 cup mixed dried fruit
50g/2oz/¼ cup glacé cherries,
   quartered
50g/2oz/⅓ cup blanched almonds,
   chopped
finely grated rind of 1 lemon
225g/8oz/1 cup almond paste
icing sugar, for dredging

1 Sift the flour and sugar. Stir in the yeast. Make a well in the centre. Warm the milk and butter, then mix with the egg into the dry ingredients.

2 Turn out the dough on to a lightly floured surface and knead for 10 minutes, until smooth and elastic. Put in a clean bowl, cover with clear film and leave in a warm place to rise for about 1 hour, or until doubled in size.

3 On a lightly floured surface, knead in the dried fruit, cherries, almonds and lemon rind.

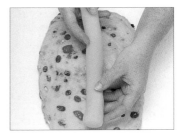

4 Roll out the dough to a rectangle about 25 x 20cm/10 x 8in. Roll the almond paste into a sausage, slightly shorter than the dough. Place in the middle of the dough. Wrap the dough around the paste.

5 Put seam side down on a greased baking sheet. Cover with oiled clear film and leave in a warm place to rise for about 40 minutes, or until doubled in size. Preheat the oven to 190°C/375°F/Gas 5.

6 Bake the stollen for 30–35 minutes, or until golden and hollow-sounding when tapped. Cool on a wire rack. Serve dusted with icing sugar.

NUTRITION NOTES

Per portion:

Energy	357Kcals/1503kJ
Protein	6.8g
Fat	14.3g
Saturated fat	5.86g
Carbohydrate	54g
Fibre	1.9g
Sodium	27mg

Sticky Chocolate, Maple and Walnut Swirls

This rich, yeasted cake breaks into separate sticky chocolate swirls, each soaked in maple syrup.

INGREDIENTS

Serves 12

450g/1lb/4 cups strong bread flour
2.5ml/½ tsp ground cinnamon
50g/2oz/4 tbsp unsalted butter
25g/1oz/2 tbsp caster sugar
1 packet easy-blend dried yeast
1 egg yolk
120ml/4fl oz/½ cup water
60ml/4 tbsp milk
45ml/3 tbsp maple syrup,
   to finish

For the filling

40g/1½oz/3 tbsps unsalted butter,
   melted
50g/2oz/¼ cup light brown sugar
175g/6oz/1 cup chocolate chips
75g/3oz/½ cup chopped walnuts

1 Grease a deep, round 23cm/9in springform cake tin. Sift the flour and cinnamon into a bowl, then cut in the butter until the mixture resembles coarse breadcrumbs.

2 Stir in the sugar and yeast. In a cup or bowl, beat the egg yolk with the water and milk, then stir into the dry ingredients to make a soft dough.

3 Knead the dough on a lightly floured surface until smooth, then roll out to a rectangle measuring about 38 x 30cm/15 x 12in.

4 For the filling, brush the dough with the melted butter and sprinkle with the sugar, chocolate chips and walnuts.

5 Roll up the dough from one long side like a Swiss roll, then cut into 12 thick, even slices.

6 Pack the slices closely together in the prepared tin, with the cut side facing upwards. Cover the dough and leave in a warm place for about 1½ hours until well risen and springy to the touch. About 15 minutes before baking, preheat the oven to 220°C/425°F/Gas 7.

7 Bake the swirls for about 30–35 minutes until well risen, golden brown and firm. Remove from the pan and cool on a wire rack. To finish, spoon or brush the maple syrup over the cake. Pull the pieces apart to serve.

NUTRITION NOTES	
Per portion:	
Energy	344Kcals/1448kJ
Protein	6.8g
Fat	14.3g
Saturated fat	5.98g
Carbohydrate	50g
Fibre	1.6g
Sodium	72mg

Moroccan Serpent Cake

This is perhaps the most famous of all Moroccan pastries, and justly so. Filled with lightly fragrant almond paste and sugar it is for special occasions only.

INGREDIENTS

Serves 8
8 sheets of filo pastry
50g/2oz/4 tbsp butter, melted
1 egg, beaten
5ml/1 tsp ground cinnamon
icing sugar, for dusting

For the almond paste
about 50g/2oz/4 tbsp unsalted butter, melted
225g/8oz/2 cups ground almonds
2.5ml/½ tsp almond essence
50g/2oz/½ cup icing sugar
egg yolk, beaten
15ml/1 tbsp rose water or orange flower water (optional)

1 First make the almond paste. Blend the melted butter with the ground almonds and almond essence. Add the sugar, egg yolk and rose or orange flower water, if using, and mix well.

COOK'S TIP

Popular in Mediterranean, Indian and Middle Eastern cuisines, the perfume from extracts of flowers or flower waters can be quite strong, so use sparingly. Very volatile, they should also be kept away from heat and light and stored in dark bottles.

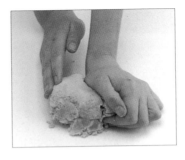

2 On a lightly floured work surface, knead until soft and pliable. Chill for about 10 minutes.

3 Break the almond paste into 10 even-size balls and roll them into 10cm/4in "sausages". Chill again.

4 Preheat the oven to 180°C/350°F/Gas 4. Place two sheets of filo pastry on the work surface so that they overlap to form an 18 x 56cm/7 x 22in rectangle. Brush the overlapping ends of the pastry to secure and then brush all over with butter. Cover with another two sheets of filo and brush again with butter.

5 Place five "sausages" of almond paste along the lower edge of the filo sheet and roll up the pastry tightly, tucking in the ends. Shape the roll into a loose coil. Repeat with the remaining filo and almond paste, so that you have two coils.

6 Brush a large baking sheet with butter and place the coils together to make a "snake".

7 Beat together the egg and half of the cinnamon. Brush over the pastry snake and then bake in the oven for 20–25 minutes until golden brown. Carefully invert the snake on to another baking sheet and return to the oven for 5–10 minutes until golden.

8 Place on a serving plate. Dust with icing sugar and then sprinkle with the remaining cinnamon. Serve warm.

NUTRITION NOTES	
Per portion:	
Energy	153Kcals/639kJ
Protein	3.1g
Fat	6.9g
Saturated fat	3.6g
Carbohydrate	21g
Fibre	.5g
Sodium	307mg

STOCKS AND BASIC RECIPES

There is a wide range of stock products, sauces and ready-made doughs on the market, but these all tend to be high in salt so it is well worth making your own at home, and having them on hand for future use. One clear advantage to making your own is that home-made products are almost always easy to make and taste better than commercial ones. Save time when making stocks by preparing a few batches and freezing them for future use. Cool the stock quickly, pour them into suitable containers (leaving space for expansion) and freeze them for up to 3 months.

CHICKEN STOCK

INGREDIENTS

Makes about 750ml/1¼ pints/3 cups
1 meaty chicken carcass
6 shallots or 1 onion, sliced
1 carrot, sliced
2 celery sticks, chopped
1 bay leaf
freshly ground black pepper

1 Break or chop the chicken carcass into pieces and place in a large saucepan with 1.75 litres/3 pints/7½ cups cold water.

2 Add the vegetables to the saucepan with the bay leaf. Stir to mix.

3 Bring to the boil, then partially cover and simmer for 2 hours. Use a slotted spoon to skim off any scum and fat that rise to the surface during cooking. Season to taste with pepper. Strain the stock through a sieve, then set aside to cool.

4 When cold, remove and discard all the fat. Cover and store in the fridge for up to 3 days.

BEEF STOCK

INGREDIENTS

Makes about 750ml/1¼ pints/3 cups
450g/1lb shin of beef on the bone
450g/1lb beef or veal bones
1 onion, sliced
1 carrot, sliced
1 turnip, diced
2 celery sticks, chopped
1 leek, chopped
handful of fresh herbs
freshly ground black pepper

1 Preheat the oven to 220°C/425°F/ Gas 7. Place the meat and bones in a roasting tin and brown in the oven for about 30 minutes.

2 Transfer the meat and bones to a large pan and pour over 1.75 litres/ 3 pints/7½ cups cold water. Add the vegetables and a handful of fresh herbs.

3 Bring to the boil, partially cover and simmer for 2 hours, skimming off any scum and fat that rise to the surface. Strain the stock, season to taste with pepper, then cool and discard any fat. Store as for chicken stock.

VEGETABLE STOCK

INGREDIENTS

Makes about 1.5 litres/2½ pints/6¼ cups
1 large onion, sliced
2 carrots, sliced
1 leek, sliced
3 celery sticks, chopped
1 small turnip, diced
1 small parsnip, sliced
1 bouquet garni
strip of lemon rind
freshly ground black pepper

1 Place all the prepared vegetables in a large saucepan with the bouquet garni. Add 1.75 litres/3 pints/7½ cups cold water and stir to mix.

2 Bring to the boil, then partially cover and gently simmer for about 1 hour, skimming off any scum. Season to taste with pepper.

3 Strain the stock through a sieve and use immediately or set aside to cool. Store in the fridge for up to 3 days. Alternatively, freeze the stock.

TOMATO SAUCE

Tomato sauce is a useful standby to have on hand in the fridge or freezer. When tomatoes are in season, make a large batch. At other times of the year, use good quality, canned whole Italian plum tomatoes.

INGREDIENTS

Makes about 600ml/1 pint/2½ cups
25g/1oz/2 tbsp unsalted butter
900g/2lb tomatoes, peeled, seeded and
   finely chopped
1.5–2.5ml/¼–½ tsp sugar
freshly ground black pepper

1 Melt the butter in a heavy-based saucepan over low heat. Add the tomatoes and stir to mix with the butter. Cover and cook for 5 minutes.

2 Uncover and stir in the sugar. Partly cover the pan and simmer gently, stirring occasionally, for 30 minutes, or until the tomatoes have softened and the sauce is thick.

3 Season the sauce to taste with pepper. Use immediately, or cool and then refrigerate or freeze.

WHITE SAUCE

A basic white sauce is an essential ingredient in many dishes, and lends itself to an endless variety of flavourings, but ready-made versions of this sauce should be avoided due to their high salt levels.

INGREDIENTS

Makes about 600ml/1 pint/2½ cups
40g/1½oz/3 tbsp unsalted butter
40g/1½oz/⅓ cup plain flour
600ml/1 pint/2½ cups milk
a generous pinch of grated nutmeg
freshly ground black pepper

1 Melt the butter in a heavy-based saucepan over low heat. Remove the pan from the heat and stir in the flour to make a smooth, soft paste.

2 Add about one-quarter of the milk and mix it in well with a whisk. When it is smooth, mix in the remaining milk.

3 Set the pan over moderately high heat and bring to the boil, whisking constantly.

4 When the sauce bubbles and starts to thicken, reduce the heat to very low and simmer the sauce gently for 5–10 minutes, whisking well from time to time. Add the grated nutmeg and season the sauce to taste with pepper. Serve hot.

RICH BROWN SAUCE

Sauce espagnole is ideal for serving with red meat and game and is a useful substitute for similar commercial products.

INGREDIENTS

Makes about 600ml/1 pint/2½ cups
25g/1oz/2tbsp unsalted butter
50g/2oz streaky bacon, chopped
2 shallots, chopped
1 carrot, chopped
1 celery stick, chopped
25g/1oz/2 tbsp plain flour
600ml/1 pint/2½ cups beef stock
1 bouquet garni
30ml/2 tbsp tomato purée
15ml/1 tbsp sherry (optional)
freshly ground black pepper

1 Melt the butter in a heavy-based saucepan and fry the bacon for 2–3 minutes. Add the vegetables and cook for a further 5–6 minutes until golden.

2 Stir in the flour and cook for 5–10 minutes until it is a rich brown colour. Remove from the heat and gradually blend in the stock.

3 Bring to the boil, continuing to stir until the sauce thickens. Add the bouquet garni, tomato purée and seasoning. Reduce the heat and simmer gently for 1 hour, stirring occasionally. Strain the sauce, pressing the vegetables to extract the juices. Skim off any fat. Stir in the sherry, if using, and adjust the seasoning to taste

MAYONNAISE

This classic combination of oil and egg yolks has thousands of uses – as an accompaniment, in sandwiches or in salad dressings.

INGREDIENTS

Makes about 350ml/12fl oz/1½ cups
2 egg yolks
350ml/12fl oz/1½ cups olive oil
15–30ml/1–2 tbsp lemon juice or
   white wine vinegar
5–10ml/1–2 tsp prepared mustard
freshly ground black pepper

1 Put the egg yolks in a bowl and beat together well.

2 Gradually add the oil 5–10ml/ 1–2 tsp at a time, beating constantly with a whisk or electric hand mixer. After one-quarter of the oil has been added very slowly and absorbed, beat in 5–10ml/1–2 tsp lemon juice or vinegar.

3 Continue beating in the oil, now in a thin, steady stream . As the mayonnaise thickens, add another 5ml/1 tsp lemon juice or vinegar.

4 When all the oil has been beaten in, add the mustard. Taste the mayonnaise and add more lemon juice or vinegar. Season with pepper. If the mayonnaise is too thick, beat in a spoonful or two of water. Home-made mayonnaise will keep, covered, in the fridge, for up to 1 week.

SAUCE BÉARNAISE

For dedicated meat eaters, this herby butter sauce adds a note of sophistication without swamping your grilled or pan-fried steak.

INGREDIENTS

Serves 2–3
45ml/3tbsp white wine vinegar
1 small onion, finely chopped
a few fresh tarragon and chervil sprigs
1 bay leaf
6 crushed black peppercorns
115g/4oz/½ cup butter
2 egg yolks
15ml/1 tbsp chopped fresh herbs, such
   as tarragon, parsley and chervil
freshly ground black pepper

1 Place the vinegar, 30ml/2 tbsp water, onion, herb sprigs and peppercorns in a saucepan. Simmer gently until the liquid is reduced by half. Strain and cool. Cream the butter until smooth.

2 In a double saucepan or a bowl set over a saucepan of gently simmering water, whisk the egg yolks and reduced liquid until light and fluffy.

3 Gradually add the butter, half a teaspoonful at a time. Whisk until all the butter has been incorporated before adding any more.

4 Add the chopped herbs and season to taste with pepper. It is best serve warm, not hot.

SPICY YOGURT MARINADE

Plan this dish well in advance; an extra-long marinating time is necessary to develop a really mellow spicy flavour.

INGREDIENTS

Serves 6
5 ml/1 tsp coriander seeds
10ml/2 tsp cumin seeds
6 cloves
2 bay leaves
1 onion, quartered
2 garlic cloves
5cm/2in piece fresh root ginger,
   peeled and roughly chopped
2.5ml/½ tsp chilli powder
5ml/1 tsp ground turmeric
150ml/¼ pint/⅔ cup plain yogurt
juice of 1 lemon
lemon or lime slices, to garnish

1 Spread the coriander and cumin seeds, cloves and bay leaves in the bottom of a large frying pan and dry-fry over a moderate heat until the bay leaves are crispy.

2 Cool the spices and grind coarsely with a pestle and mortar.

3 Finely mince the onion, garlic and ginger in a food processor or blender. Add the ground spices, chilli powder, turmeric, yogurt and lemon juice. Garnish with lemon slices.

BASIC PIZZA DOUGH

This simple bread base is rolled out thinly for a traditional pizza recipe.

INGREDIENTS

Makes 4 x 13cm/5in round pizza bases, or 1 x 30 x 18cm/12 x 7in oblong pizza base, or 1 x 4–4½cm/10–12in round pizza base
175g/6oz/1½ cups strong bread flour
1 tsp easy-blend dried yeast
120–150ml/4–5fl oz/½–⅔ cups
   lukewarm water
15ml/1 tbsp olive oil

1 Sift the flour into a large mixing bowl and stir in the yeast. Make a well in the centre and pour in the water and oil. Mix to a soft dough.

2 Knead the dough on a lightly floured surface for about 10 minutes until smooth and elastic.

3 Place the dough in a greased bowl and cover with clear film. Leave to rise in a warm place for about 1 hour, or until the dough has doubled in size.

4 Knock back the dough. Turn out on to a lightly floured surface and knead again for 2–3 minutes. Roll out as required and place on a greased baking sheet. Pinch up the dough to make a rim. The dough is now ready for topping.

SHORTCRUST PASTRY

A meltingly short, crumbly pastry sets off any filling to perfection, whether sweet or savoury. For a lower-fat version, the pastry dough can be made with half butter or margarine and half white vegetable fat or entirely with one kind of fat.

INGREDIENTS

Makes 1 x 23cm/9in pastry case
225g/8oz/2 cups plain flour
115g/4oz/½ cup unsalted butter
45–60ml/3–4 tbsp iced water

1 Sift the flour into a bowl. Add the fat. Rub it into the flour with your fingertips until the mixture resembles fine breadcrumbs.

2 Sprinkle 45ml/3 tbsp water over the mixture. With a fork, toss gently to mix and moisten it.

3 Press the dough into a ball. If it is too dry to form a dough, add the remaining water.

4 Wrap the ball of dough with clear film or greaseproof paper and chill for at least 30 minutes before rolling out. Store in the fridge for up to three days in clear film, or up to three months in the freezer.

FRENCH FLAN PASTRY

The pastry for tarts, flans and quiches is made with butter or margarine, giving a rich and crumbly result.

INGREDIENTS

Makes 1 x 23cm/9in flan case
7oz/200g/1¼ cups plain flour
115g/4oz/½ cup unsalted butter or
   margarine, chilled
1 egg yolk
1.5ml/¼ tsp lemon juice
30–45ml/2–3 tbsp iced water

1 Sift the flour into a bowl. Add the butter or margarine. Rub the fat into the flour until the mixture resembles fine breadcrumbs.

2 In a small bowl, mix the egg yolk, lemon juice and 30ml/2 tbsp water. Add to the flour mixture. With a fork, toss gently to mix and moisten.

3 Press the dough into a rough ball. If it is too dry to come together, add the remaining water. Turn on to a work surface or pastry board.

4 With the heel of your hand, push portions of dough away from you, on to the surface. Continue in this way until the dough feels pliable and can be peeled easily off the surface.

5 Press the dough into a smooth ball. Wrap in clear film and chill for at least 30 minutes before use.

INDEX